For all hockey fans...

DETROIT RED WINGS

Hockeytown USA Trivia, Fun and Games

Bob and H.W. Kondras

Blue River Press
Indianapolis, IN

Cover designed by Phil Velikan
Cover photo: USPRESSWIRE.COM/Michael Sackett
Editorial assistance provided by Dorothy Chambers
Packaged by Wish Publishing

Printed in the United States of America
10 9 8 7 6 5 4 3 2

Published by Blue River Press
Distributed by Cardinal Publishers Group
Tom Doherty Company, Inc.
www.cardinalpub.com

Table of Contents

1

The Early Years
1926-1939

There were 11 bids for NHL franchises from American cities at the 1926 spring meetings; five were from Detroit. One of the groups had even tried to buy the Edmonton franchise and move it to the Motor City, so an NHL team coming to town seemed inevitable.

And so it was, the francise was awarded to a group that included former Ottawa Silver Seven and Toronto Blueshirts goalkeeper Percy LeSuer. The franchise acquired the rights to the players from the WHL's Victoria Cougars, and the Detroit Cougars came into being. The first player/manager was Art Duncan, who had led the 1923-24 Pacific Coast Hockey Association in scoring with Vancouver.

As they did not yet have an arena in Detroit, the team played their first season in Windsor, Ontario, making the Detroit Cougars the first professional sports team to play its home games in a foreign country. A disappointing first season in many ways, the Cougars finished 12-28-4.

The next season brought two significant changes. First, the team hired a new manager, Jack Adams. Second, the Olympia–Detroit's own rink–was finally ready. The team could actually play at home in their own city.

In their first seven seasons, Detroit made the playoffs only twice and lost in the first round on both occasions. A name change in 1930 to the Detroit Falcons proved to be unhelpful. They were no more victorious as birds than they had been as cats.

However, in 1932 the team was purchased by grain millionaire Jack Norris. It was Norris who changed the team's name to the Red Wings and suggested that a winged wheel—which had been the logo of the first Stanley Cup winning team, the Winged Wheelers–would be a perfect fit for the team in Detroit.

With some clever player acquisitions and better funding, the team was able to make it to the Stanley Cup semi-finals the first season that Norris owned the team. They were the first American-based franchise to win back-to-back Stanley Cup championships in 1936 and 1937, but they did not make the playoffs in 1938 and were out in the semifinals in 1939.

Wilf Cude Sudoku

Use logic to fill in the boxes so each row, column and 2x4 box contain the letters W-I-L-F-C-U-D-E to celebrate Wilf Cude, a 1933-34 midseason goalie acquisition from the Montreal Canadiens. Solution on page 111.

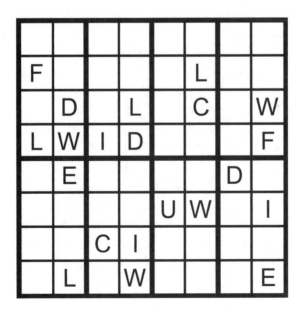

Find Some Wings

```
B  S  R  E  H  C  A  N  O  C  E  I  L  R  A  H  C
X  T  E  S  G  E  I  P  M  T  N  J  A  A  A  R  N
E  A  G  E  N  A  C  W  Q  Z  T  D  R  F  L  E  O
W  E  N  M  U  N  A  C  N  U  D  T  R  A  E  P  T
O  K  O  L  O  T  R  S  P  U  O  E  Y  F  C  O  S
H  E  B  O  Y  Y  L  I  K  S  S  H  A  T  C  O  Y
D  K  L  H  G  Y  V  B  N  Q  E  N  U  C  O  C  O
Y  U  E  P  U  Q  O  T  W  R  Q  M  R  U  N  N  F
S  D  A  A  O  H  S  M  B  Y  B  L  I  G  N  O  K
E  Q  U  H  D  N  S  I  W  J  N  M  E  A  E  S  N
J  A  C  K  S  T  E  W  A  R  T  B  C  K  L  R  A
Y  O  G  Y  O  L  N  S  I  D  A  B  E  L  L  A  R
E  B  B  I  E  G  O  O  D  F  E  L  L  O  W  C  F
A  I  U  W  C  O  O  N  E  Y  W  E  I  L  A  N  D
H  L  I  G  E  O  R  G  E  H  A  Y  T  V  U  A  P
Q  S  T  I  N  Y  T  H  O  M  P  S  O  N  B  M  U
X  H  L  L  D  Q  L  J  T  S  E  G  T  R  H  M  R
```

Solutions on page 111.

ALEC CONNELL
ART DUNCAN
CARL VOSS
CARSON COOPER
CHARLIE CONACHER
COONEY WEILAND
DOUG YOUNG
DUKE KEATS
EBBIE GOODFELLOW
FRANK FOYSTON

GEORGE HAY
HAP HOLMES
HERBIE LEWIS
JACK STEWART
LARRY AURIE
REG NOBLE
SID ABEL
SYD HOWE
TINY THOMPSON

In the Beginning ...

Solutions on page 112.

Across

9 Oracle (4-3)

10 WHL owners who sold out to the NHL in 1926: Lester and Frank _____ (7)

11 Toronto team that beat Detroit in the 1929 Stanley Cup playoffs (7)

12 Defeated by the Red Wings in the 1936 Stanley Cup finals (7)

13 Special ___ (3)

14 Skate essential (5)

16 Spent 11 seasons with Detroit and was considered to be the heart and soul of the franchise. (5)

19 Team that Detroit originally acquired players from: Victoria _____ (7)

22 Detroit team name in 1930 (7)

24 Came to the Detroit team in 1927 and stayed for 36 years (5)

26 Hockey hit (5)

28 "Wheels" (3)

30 Site of all first year home games for the Detroit team (7)

33 Masked mammal (7)

35 Scored 21 goals in 47 games in 1934 (7)

36 Trainee (7)

Down

1 With hands on hips (6)

2 Visionary owner of the Red Wings from 1932-1952 (6)

3 ___ Bell (4)

4 Panhandle site (6)

5 Clash (4)

6 Breastbones (6)

7 Animal with a mane (4)

8 Greek school of art and design (4)

14 ___ constrictor (3)

15 North Pole toymaker (3)

17 *Winnie the Pooh* baby (3)

18 Dash lengths (3)

19 When doubled, a dance (3)

20 ___ *Today* (3)

21 "Hold on a ___!" (3)

23 Albanian coin (3)

25 Nun

27 Detroit was the first NHL team to play on this continent (6)

28 Led the team in scoring in 1929 (6)

29 Kitchen appliances (6)

30 Desire (4)

31 "Cheers" regular (4)

32 Bank (4)

34 Karate blow (4)

The early years: How well do you know them?

1. In 1926, there were two divisions in the NHL: Canadian and American. Can you name the 10 teams?

2. There were a variety of important rules created in the 1930s that affected the game for good. Can you name two?

3. How many games were played in the NHL regular season from 1926-1931?

4. Who was the first Detroit player to make it into the top 10 scorers for the season?

5. Larry Aurie, the legendary Detroit winger, was also known by these nicknames.

6. Aurie's number was officially retired by James Norris after the 1937-38 season. Does it hang in the rafters at Joe Louis Arena?

7. Can you name the four professional hockey teams that Jack Adams played for as a player?

8. Hall-of-Famer George Hay played for seven seasons with Detroit and was known for his superior stickhandling. After retiring as a player in 1933, he went on to coach. Which team?

9. What was the name of the Windsor arena that was home to the Detroit Cougars for the 1926-27 season?

10. What two teams did James Norris try to purchase prior to buying the Detroit franchise?

11. Who is the James Norris trophy awarded to?

Solutions on pages 112-113.

Legendary Red Wings: 1926-1939

Solutions on page 113.

Across

1 Scarf material (4)

3 "Aquarius" musical (4)

6 Bar offering (5)

10 Clinch, with "up" (3)

11 Accessory (5)

12 Olympic swimmer Janet (5)

13 Discomfit (5)

14 Dynamic duo with Tracy (7)

15 Nickname for Red Wing Cecil Thompson (4)

17 AKA "Shovel Shot," this Detroit Cougar and Falcon went on to be chief scout for the Red Wings: Carson _____. (6)

19 Red Wing Modere Bruneteau was known by this nickname. (3)

22 After seven seasons, this Cougar became coach of the Detroit Olympics after retiring from playing: George ____. (3)

23 Baseball segment (6)

24 Born in Wales, this Red Wing goaltender helped the team win their first Stanley Cup: ___ Cude (4)

26 In the center of things (7)

29 In ___ (not yet born) (5)

31 His nickname was "Goal-A-Game": Marty ____. (5)

32 Baghdad resident (5)

33 Ascap alternative (3)

34 Correct, as text (5)

35 Attention (4)

36 Bungle, with "up" (4)

Down

1 AKA Bigfoot (9)

2 This left winger was inducted into the Hall of Fame in 1989 but played for the Wings in the '30s. (5)

4 P.M. (9)

5 The goaltender was also known as "Little Napoleon" and "The Port Perry Cucumber": John Ross ____. (5)

6 This player led the Detroit Cougars in goals (13), assists (8) and penalty minutes (60) during their inaugural season: Johnny _____. (8)

7 Big mess (5)

8 "A Doll's House" playwright (5)

9 Known as "Duke," he played for the Detroit Cougars from 1926-1928. (5)

16 "Uh-uh" (3)

18 Stab (9)

19 "Who, me?" (3)

20 Jonquils (9)

21 Innocent (4-4)

25 This right winger was also known as "Little Dempsey": Larry ____ (5)

26 This Red Wing was the last active player from the NHL's first season and the 1910s. (5)

27 Bad language (5)

28 This Red Wing goalie had 92 saves in a 176-minute game against the Montreal Maroons: Normie ____. (5)

30 Nicknamed "Poker Face," this Red Wing was with the team for 14 seasons: _____ Goodfellow (5)

Red Wings You Should Know: George Hay

George Hay had already enjoyed a fairly lengthy professional career before he entered the NHL and became known as the "best stickhandler in hockey." He turned pro in 1921 with the Regina Cups and continued to play in the Western Canada Hockey League until it collapsed in 1926. He, along with many others from the team, went to the Chicago Black Hawks for their first season and was then traded to Detroit for the 1927-28 season. He led the team in scoring and earned a spot on the all-star team that was then determined by the NHL's 10 coaches. Hay remained in Detroit until 1934. He was elected to the Hockey Hall of Fame in 1958.

2

The 1940s

The '40s started well for the Red Wings; they made the Stanley Cup Finals for three consecutive years at the beginning of the decade. In the 1941 series, they were swept by the Boston Bruins. In '42, they lost in a seven-game series to Toronto after winning the first three games. The series is also notable for being the first time a coach was suspended in a final. Red Wings coach Jack Adams was so enraged by what he perceived to be biased penalty calls that violence ensued — a referee ended up punched in the nose. The Leafs' comeback from a three-game deficit and ultimate victory is still referred to as one of THE great comebacks in sports.

But in '43, everything came together, and Detroit won its third Stanley Cup by sweeping the Bruins. They went on to make it into the playoffs every year for the decade and even made it back to the finals three times.

Perhaps the most important event of the '40s, however, was the arrival in 1946 of Gordie Howe. Howe began slowly, only scoring seven goals and racking up 15 assists his first season, but he went on to be a true hockey legend. By Howe's second season, he was part of the "Production Line" with Ted Lindsay and Sid Abel. This high scoring trio would lead the Wings to the Stanley Cup Finals in '48 and '49, only to be beaten by Toronto both years.

Also in '46, Jack Adams stepped aside as head coach of the Red Wings to focus on being the team's general manager. He was replaced by minor league coach Tommy Ivan. Adams had led the team to three Stanley Cups. Much later, in 1974, the NHL honored Adams by creating the Jack Adams Award which is given to the most outstanding coach in the league every year.

Gordie Howe Sudoku

Use logic to fill in the boxes so each row, column and 2x4 box contain the letters G-O-R-D-I-E to celebrate Gordie Howe, a true Red Wings legend. Solution on page 114.

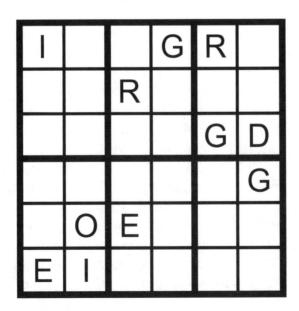

The 1943 Stanley Cup Winners

Hidden in the grid below are the members of the 1942-43 Red Wings that won the Stanley Cup. See if you can find them all. Solution is on page 114.

```
J L D O U G L A S S J D F M W
A I W T R A W E T S N A X R O
C S U A E T E N U R B H L E L
K C C Z E J O N B A N O E E L
S O Q T H S O R O E T W B T E
O M G V R T G F L M H E A A F
N B J H F B E N T A I L Z C D
B E W I D C M V I B N S I M O
A T O L O H O A R N X D G N O
O K U O W O N O F A N Y O I G
S A Q A M O W E R S C E I S T
N V R U K N G R O S S O J H V
K E Q U A C K E N B U S H U M
S J T U C R E H S I F V J E R
M O T T E R K P W A T S O N O
```

ABEL	GROSSO	MOWERS
BEHLING	HOLOTA	ORLANDO
BROWN	HOWE	QUACKENBUSH
BRUNETEAU	JACKSON	SIMON
CARVETH	JENNINGS	STEWART
DOUGLAS	LISCOMBE	WARES
FISHER	MCATEE	WATSON
GOODFELLOW	MOTTER	

The Fabulous '40s

Solutions on page 115.

Across

1 Response to the captain (3-3)

5 Detroit Hall of Famer Roy _____, inducted in 1998 (8)

9 Referee who was the cause of Jack Adams' suspension in the 1942 Stanley Cup Finals (7)

10 Cried, like when your team loses ... (6)

11 Hockey great who joined the Red Wings in 1946 (6,4)

12 Bit of physics (4)

14 Third generation of hockey players (8)

17 Standout Red Wing goalie who started with the team during the '44-45 season. (6)

19 Improper user (6)

21 *Dangerous* ____ (8)

23 "What are the ___?" (4)

25 AKA "Snowshoes," this former left winger and coach was considered by some to be the greatest fighter in the NHL. (10)

28 She wore an itsy-bitsy, teeny-weeny, yellow-polka-dotted one (6)

30 Marathoner's or hockey player's need (7)

31 Way to compete for the puck in the face-off (8)

32 Minuscule (6)

Down

2 What you say when your team wins the Stanley Cup (5)

3 Bitter (5)

4 Runaway brides and grooms (7)

5 Native American language family (7)

6 FDR's policy platform (3,4)

7 Fine dinnerware (5)

8 Adam's madam (3)

13 Arctic ___ (5)

15 Fanatical, like a Red Wings fan (5)

16 Discouraging words (3)

18 "___ Miniver" (3)

20 This came into being in the NHL in 1943; some call it the beginning of the game's "modern era." (3,4)

21 AKA "Terrible Ted," this Red Wings forward is in the HHOF (7)

22 Inflexible (7)

24 Downhill racer (5)

26 Drink garnish (5)

27 Dutch exports (5)

29 "Rocky ___" (3)

How well do you know your 1940 Red Wings?

1. Who was the goaltender that Jack Adams traded in 1937 to Toronto that ended up being a leader in that team's 1942 victory over Detroit in the Stanley Cup?

2. This player became the team's (then) all-time leading scorer on January 23, 1944 with a hat trick against the New York Rangers.

3. The NHL allowed its teams club rights to all players within a 50-mile radius of an NHL city before the draft was instituted, which was good news for some teams but not as good for others. As a result-only three teams won the Stanley Cup between 1942 and 1960. Name them.

4. The "Production Line" finished in the top three for NHL scoring in the 1949-50 season. Who were the three players?

5. What is the name of the Boston goalie who led the sweep of the Red Wings in the 1941 Stanley Cup Finals?

6. Both Sid Abel and Jack Stewart served in this military organization from 1943-1945.

7. Who became the Red Wings coach in 1947?

8. This Red Wing was 1947's Rookie of the Year and went on to win of three Vezina Trophies.

9. This former Red Wing played on more Stanley Cup-winning teams (eight) than any player who did NOT play for the Montreal Canadiens.

10. He won the Art Ross Trophy for the 1949-1950 season.

11. What is a "Gordie Howe Hat Trick"?

12. How many Gordie Howe Hat Tricks did Gordie Howe have during his career?

Solutions on page 115.

Legendary Red Wings: The 1940s

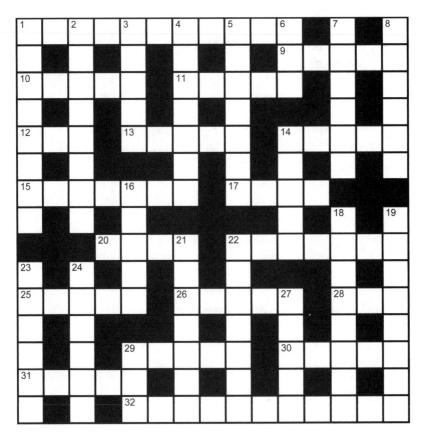

Solutions on page 116.

Across

1 First defenseman to win the Lady Byng Trophy (11)

9 Boo-boo (5)

10 Djinn (5)

11 "Holy smokes!" (5)

12 Tease (3)

13 Sleep on it (5)

14 AKA "The Flying Scotsman": Adam _____ (5)

15 Defenseman known as "Black Jack": John _____ (7)

17 Holds the record for fastest overtime goal scored in NHL history, at 25 seconds: Syd _____ (4)

20 Known as "Old Bootnose": Sid _____ (4)

22 Saloon (7)

25 Blush (5)

26 Cupid's projectile (5)

28 "60 Minutes" network (3)

29 Beyond's partner (5)

30 Buzz (5)

31 Floor it (5)

32 In stock (3-3-5)

Down

1 Speediest (8)

2 Not all there (8)

3 Toys with tails (5)

4 Ignore (7)

5 Open (7)

6 Attention-getter (3)

7 Prayer (6)

8 Familiarize (6)

14 First round pick for the Red Wings in 1992 (22nd overall): Curtis _____ (5)

16 Mosey (5)

18 Last surviving member of the 1943 Stanley Cup team: Carl _____ (8)

19 Undecorated type (8)

21 A little off base (4,3)

22 Right wing who won two Stanley Cups with the Red Wings (1943 and 1950) (7)

23 Red Wing forward who also played for the Bruins and the Black Hawks (6)

24 Goalie who was also known as "Apple Cheeks": Harry _____ (6)

27 Right wing who played for the Red Wings on and off between 1938-43 (5)

29 "Much ___ About Nothing" (3)

Red Wings You Should Know:
Sid Abel

Originally from Melville, Saskatchewan, Sid "Old Bootnose" Abel was an important part of the Red Wings' famous "Production Line." He won the Hart Trophy as the NHL's most valuable player for his play in 1949 and contributed solidly to the team until he was traded to the Black Hawks for the 1952-53 season. He came back to the Wings for the 1957-58 season as a player and in 1969-70 as a coach.

Elected to the Hall of Fame in 1969, Sid went on after retiring as a player coach to be a color commentator for Red Wings broadcasts on TV and radio through much of the 1970s and 80s. He was ranked number 85 on the 1998 *Hockey News* list of the 100 greatest hockey players. Impressive!

3
The 1950s

Detroit started off the '50s in a big way with its "Production Line" of Gordie Howe, Ted Lindsay and Sid Abel finishing at the top of NHL scoring for the 1949-50 season and then going on to beat the Rangers in the Stanley Cup Finals. After the game, Ted Lindsay skated around the Olympia stadium holding the Stanley Cup — a tradition that continues to this day. Gordie Howe suffered a severe head injury early in the series when he tried to check Teeder Kennedy and missed ... running head-first into the boards. *Total Hockey* quotes Howe as saying, "I enjoyed my last three Stanley Cups ... I don't remember much about the first one."

Those other three Stanley Cups would come in quick succession — '52, '54 and '55. All three victories came at the expense of the Montreal Canadiens. The 1952 series is best remembered for being the first time in NHL history that the Stanley Cup winners came through the playoffs with a perfect record, 8-0. Terry Sawchuck, Detroit's goalie at the time and considered by some to be one of the game's greatest, had four shutouts during the playoffs.

Other notable additions to the team in the '50s included Bob Goldham, Marcel Pronovost, Pete Babando, Tony Leswick and Alex Delvecchio. Departures included that of Ted Lindsay, who was traded to Chicago in 1957 along with Glenn Hall after trying to start the National Hockey League Players association. Sawchuck was traded away in

'55 to Boston, but then traded back for in '58. The Red Wings were swept by the Bruins in the first round of the playoffs that year. And in 1959, they missed the playoffs entirely for the first time in 21 years.

Terry Sawchuk Sudoku

Use logic to fill in the boxes so each row, column and 2x4 box contain the letters T-S-A-W-C-H-U-K to celebrate Terry Sawchuck, one of Detroits greats in goal. Solution on page 116.

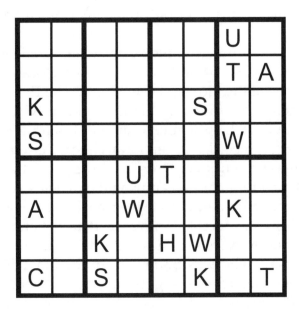

The Undefeated-in-the-Playoffs '52 Stanley Cup Champions

L	R	L	M	H	K	R	L	W	T	V	M	P
D	E	L	V	E	C	C	H	I	O	A	I	E
Y	I	W	R	D	O	I	B	A	H	I	A	R
T	S	V	O	K	S	B	L	D	L	F	T	X
X	E	N	J	H	S	B	L	E	S	L	S	V
P	R	O	N	O	V	O	S	T	V	A	Y	T
N	J	S	J	G	G	W	A	Y	W	A	R	C
Y	L	L	E	K	I	S	A	C	R	B	P	Y
E	E	I	C	C	I	S	H	O	E	E	L	S
S	D	W	K	U	D	U	Q	F	V	L	W	V
G	I	J	K	N	K	M	U	L	O	P	I	R
Z	E	H	I	Z	Z	I	S	I	L	C	S	A
R	Z	L	K	L	T	O	C	N	G	P	C	I

Solutions on page 117.

ABEL	PRONOVOST
COFLIN	PRYSTAI
DELVECCHIO	REISE
GLOVER	SAWCHUK
GOLDHAM	SCLISIZZI
HALL	SKOV
HOWE	STASIUK
KELLY	TIBBS
LESWICK	WILSON
LINDSAY	WOIT
PAVELICH	ZEIDEL

The Nifty Fifties

Solutions on page 117.

Across

1 Wow (6)

4 Chachi always wore one. (8)

9 Well known (5)

10 Glower (5)

11 "Baloney!" (3)

12 Red Wings coach from 1947-54 (4)

13 Pepsi rival (4)

14 Kick out (5)

16 Three-time Stanley Cup winning goaltender (7)

17 Diplomacy (4)

18 Biblical suffix (3)

21 Team captain for '52 Stanley Cup winners (4)

22 Embodiment (7)

25 Bacteria discovered by Theodor Escherich (1,4)

26 "I'll second that." (4)

27 What dwarves say when they go to work (5)

28 "___ alive!" (3)

29 Often-missed humor (5)

30 Misspelling of Red Wings back-up goalie on the Stanley Cup (4,4)

31 Dangerous (6)

Down

1 Warner Brothers duck's claim to fame (8)

2 African nation (8)

3 Disney dog (4)

5 Domicile (5)

6 Hall of Famer who played for the Red Wings from 1952-73 (10)

7 Team owner who died in 1952 (6)

8 Keen (6)

10 Coral reef activity (7)

15 "_____ are coming!" (2 words) (3,7)

17 "___ hangs a tale ..." (7)

19 Team captain for '52 Stanley Cup losers (8)

20 Red Wing who served as a member of Parliament from 1962-1965 (3,5)

23 Betsy Ross activity (6)

24 Tiny tree (6)

26 Run ___ of (5)

27 Number nine (4)

The 1950s – How well do you know them?

1. Why was the entire 1950 Stanley Cup Final series between the Rangers and the Red Wings played in Detroit?

2. The 1950-51 season started with Detroit making the biggest trade in NHL history. Who did they trade, who did they trade for, and finally, what team did they trade with?

3. How many goals did Terry Sawchuk allow on home ice during the 1952 Stanley Cup playoffs?

4. What former Red Wing became a player coach for the Chicago Black Hawks during the '52-'53 season?

5. Who was the first NHL player to win the James Norris Memorial Trophy for best defenseman?

6. How many Stanley Cups were won by the Canadiens during the 1950s?

7. The first televised NHL game was on October 8, 1950. Who played and where?

8. Name the Red Wing who was the long time record holder in the NHL for most consecutive games played, with 580.

9. Who was the first NHL player to win the Art Ross Trophy three times in 1953?

10. What made its first NHL appearance on March 10, 1955?

11. Whose record did Gordie Howe break in 1957 with his 409th assist?

12. Who became the coach of the Red Wings in 1958?

13. What made its first appearance on the ice on April 15, 1952 when thrown by Pete and Jerry Cusimano?

Solutions on page 118.

Legendary Red Wings: The 1950s

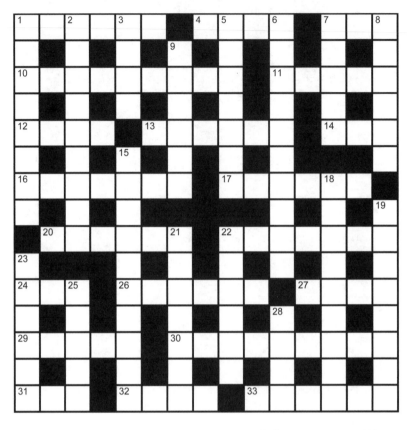

Solutions on page 118.

Across

1 Official documents (6)

4 Patriotic symbol (4)

7 Cold and wet (3)

10 Infringement (9)

11 Architectural projection (5)

12 Animal with a mane (4)

13 On the back (6)

14 "I" problem (3)

16 *Love in the Time of* _____ (7)

17 Flunky (3-3)

20 Kitchen appliances (6)

22 Part of three Red Wing teams that brought home the Stanley Cup, this player was known as "Golden Boy." (7)

24 "A rat!" (3)

26 Western hero (6)

27 Mr. Hockey (4)

29 Slender woman (5)

30 Everybody (9)

31 Cunning (3)

32 Adjective often applied to Chardonnay (4)

33 Add (6)

Down

1 This left wing spent 10 years in a Red Wings uniform and is considered one of the best defensive forwards of all time. (8)

2 Five-time Stanley Cup-winning defenseman who was inducted into the HHOF in 1978. (9)

3 Drift (4)

5 AKA "Terrible Ted" (7)

6 Evil-looking pumpkins can be said to have been carved _____. (10)

7 First son to follow his father into the NHL: Leo ____ Jr. (5)

8 Four-time winner of the Stanley Cup as a player, this Red Wing went on to coach the team in 1971. (6)

9 Brunch beverage (6)

15 Member of the Production Line, known as "Fats" (10)

18 Greek goddess of love (9)

19 Stuck in (8)

21 Red Wing legend in goal, AKA "Ukey" (7)

22 Sad (6)

23 Against (6)

25 This player was on eight Stanley Cup-winning teams: four with Detroit and four with Toronto. (5)

28 Become unhinged (4)

Red Wings You Should Know:
Terry Sawchuk

Terry Sawchuk led the Red Wings to three Stanley Cups, won the Calder Trophy for Rookie of the Year and three Vezina Trophies for fewest goals allowed. He was selected as an All-Star five times in his first five years in the NHL. He also had more than 400 stitches in his face before adopting a protective face mask in 1962.

During his career, Sawchuk won more than 500 games (447 regular season and 54 playoff games), recorded 115 shutouts, and set the standard for NHL goalies. He was posthumously elected to the Hockey Hall of Fame and awarded the Lester Patrick Trophy in 1971.

4
Gordie Howe

How can you have a book about the Detroit Red Wings without devoting a chapter to "Mr. Hockey"? You can't

Gordon Howe (AKA "Power," "Mr. Everything," "Mr. All-Star," "The Most," "The Great Gordie," "The King of Hockey," "The Legend," "The Man," "No. 9" and "Mr. Elbows") was born March 31, 1928. He is the only player to have played in the NHL for five decades. He won four Stanley Cups with the Red Wings, six Hart Trophies for being the NHL's most valuable player and six Art Ross Trophies for being the league's leading scorer. He was the first-ever recipient of the NHL Lifetime Achievement Award.

Howe started his career at 16 when he was signed by the Red Wings and assigned to their junior team, the Galt Red Wings. He then was sent to the Omaha Knights of the USHL at 17 before starting with the Detroit Red Wings in 1946. He wore the number 17 his rookie year, but when offered the opportunity to take 9 after Roy Conacher was traded to the Black Hawks, he jumped at it. (The lower number meant he would get a lower bunk on the trains when they traveled.)

Howe was known for being a great scorer, a playmaker and a big-time fighter. A "Gordie Howe Hat Trick" consists of a goal, an assist and a fight in the same game. He finished in the top five in scoring for 20 straight seasons and scored 20+ goals in 22 consecutive seasons, an NHL record.

After retiring in 1971 due to wrist problems, Howe worked in the Red Wings front office until 1974 when he was offered the opportunity to play with the World Hockey Association's Houston Aeros, who had already signed his two sons, Mark and Marty. He had surgery for his wrist and then went on to lead the Aeros to two consecutive championships. In 1977, he left Houston to play with the New England Whalers, where he remained until the WHA folded in '79 and the team became the NHL Hartford Whalers.

In 1980, at age 51, Howe played in all 80 games, scored 15 goals and helped the team make the playoffs before retiring a second time. He returned for one game with the IHL Detroit Vipers in 1997 and played one shift. As a result, he is the only player to have played in six decades as a professional between the 1940s and the 1990s.

The Details

- 23-time NHL All-Star
- Four-time Stanley Cup champion ('50, '52, '54, '55)
- Six-time Art Ross Memorial Trophy winner ('51, '52, '53, '54, '57, '63)
- Six-time Hart Memorial Trophy winner ('52, '53, '57, '58, '60, '63,
- Lester B. Patrick Award winner (1967)
- Lionel Conacher Award (1963)
- Hockey Hall of Fame (1972)
- Two-time AVCO World Trophy winner ('74, '75)
- Gary L. Davidson Trophy winner (1974)
- Two-time WHA All-Star
- Top five in NHL scoring for 20 consecutive seasons
- Most games played for a single franchise (1687, Detroit Red Wings)
- Most goals (786) and points (1809) with a single franchise (Detroit Red Wings)
- Most NHL games played (1767)
- Oldest NHL player at retirement (52), and oldest player to play in an NHL game. Only player to play after age 50.
- Only player to play in the NHL in five different decades.
- NHL Lifetime Achievement Award (2008)
- His number 9 has been retired by
  - Detroit Red Wings
  - New England/Hartford Whalers/Carolina Hurricanes
  - Houston Aeros
- Ranked #3 on the 100 Greatest Hockey Players by *The Hockey News*

Mr. Hockey

Solutions on page 119.

Across

1 One of Howe's greatest tools on the ice was that he was _____. (12)

10 Mrs. Hockey (7)

11 A hockey fan's favorite cup (7)

12 Howe's USHL team: _____ Knights (5)

15 Trophy awarded to Howe in 1974 (8)

17 Howe, Lindsay and Abel: The _____ Line (10)

19 Howe's junior team: _____ Red Wings (4)

21 Son that was inducted into the Hall of Fame in 2011 (4)

23 Supply and demand (4,6)

25 Opposite of shortness (8)

28 Coach who supposedly said to Howe, "I know you can fight. Now show me you can play hockey." (5)

32 Idolized Howe as a youngster (7)

33 Knocked out by Howe as a rookie with one punch. (7)

35 Birthplace of Howe (12)

Down

2 Kind of toast (5)

3 Rink surface (3)

4 A long, long time (4)

5 10 kilogauss (5)

6 King that converted the Norse to Christianity (4,1)

7 AKA the Dead Sea (4,3)

8 Bounce back, in a way (4)

9 Baby swan (6)

13 Fold, spindle or mutilate (3)

14 Grad (4)

16 Awaken (4)

18 Comply with (4)

20 Astronaut's insignia (4)

21 Distance between two points (6)

22 First NHL team to offer Howe a tryout (7)

24 *A Nightmare on ___ Street* (3)

26 Indiana Jones' nemesis (5)

27 Ancient Phoenician city (5)

29 Manila hemp (5)

30 Cola (4)

31 Dundee to a friend? (4)

34 Pool tool (3)

Howe about a little trivia?

1. Gordie Howe played his first NHL game on October 16, 1946. Against what team did he play?

2. Did he get into a fight?

3. On March 3, 1959, the Red Wings held a "Gordie Howe Night" to present Howe with a special gift. What was it?

4. How many games did Howe play in to reach the 1000-point mark?

5. Whose record(s) for longevity did Howe break in 1966?

6. Who came close to Howe's record for NHL games played but retired with 11 less?

7. Who was Howe trying to check when he missed and suffered the worst injury of his career in the 1950 playoffs?

Solutions on page 119.

5
The 1960s

The 1960s were not a great decade for the Red Wings. They reached the Stanley Cup Finals four times—in 1961, 1963, 1964 and 1966 — but lost in each series. In 1961, they faced off against the Chicago Black Hawks in the first-ever all U.S. final. In '63 and '64 they lost to the Toronto Maple Leafs, and in '66 they were bested by the Canadiens, despite goalie Roger Crozier winning the Conn Smythe Trophy as playoff MVP.

The biggest change in the league during the '60s was the addition of six more teams, doubling its size, for the 1967-68 season. The Philadelphia Flyers, Los Angeles Kings, St. Louis Blues, Minnesota North Stars, Pittsburgh Penguins and Oakland Seals all debuted, and the league was split into two six-team divisions. The "Original Six" became the East Division, and the new teams (despite location) became the West. The season increased to 74 games with 50 played within a team's division. The top four in each division made the playoffs.

The best news for Detroit fans during the decade was Gordie Howe breaking Maurice "Rocket" Richard's record for the most career NHL goals on November 10, 1963. Howe scored his 545th goal against Charlie Hodge and the Canadiens.

Ron Murphy Sudoku

Use logic to fill in the boxes so each row, column and 2x4 box contain the letters M-U-R-P-H-Y to celebrate Ron Murphy, who played two seasons in the '60s with the team. Solution on page 120.

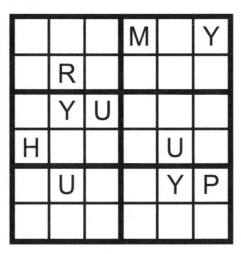

Murray Oliver Sudoku

Use logic to fill in the boxes so each row, column and 2x4 box contain the letters O-L-I-V-E-R to celebrate Murray Oliver, who played three seasons with the Red Wings. Solution on page 120.

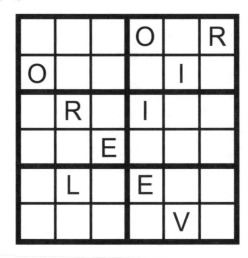

More than 20 Goals in a Season in the '60s

```
R B E N R H O W I E G L O V E R H
N O R M U L L M A N I Q N Q C C X
Z I G A R R Y U N G E R H R I H D
Q H O E Q M I V T Z O N N L T L L
W C R W R U U Z T N S O V I N L A
N C D L T G Q R M Q S O M D E Z N
K E I H H K C U R R H S C Y R E O
K V E K U Q R A E A D O X U P Y D
L L H B I P D D M Y Y S L E N U C
Z E O U H K N S O E L O G Q A I A
Y D W Y K E I L F L C X L P E P M
I X E I H C F O G V P U M I D C R
K E A L N Q Z R A E X N R R V M E
H L U A I M B U X K M P V B I E K
G A R Y A L D C O R N U T T D C R
P F X R G C H V V V E Q Z Z M I A
P W E I K S W O K M E T S E T E P
```

Solutions on page 121.

ALEX DELVECCHIO

BRUCE MACGREGOR

DEAN PRENTICE

FLOYD SMITH

FRANCIS MAHOVLICH

GARRY UNGER

GARY ALDCORN

GORDIE HOWE

HOWIE GLOVER

MURRAY OLIVER

NORM ULLMAN

PARKER MACDONALD

PAUL HENDERSON

PETE STEMKOWSKI

RON MURPHY

The Slightly Sad '60s

Solutions on page 121.

Across

7 Baker's dozen? (5)

8 Ecuador islands (9)

10 Led the league in 1964-65 with 42 goals but missed out on the overall scoring title by four points to Stan Mikita (6)

11 Camper's supply (8)

12 Like the 1942 Stanley Cup Finals — losing after winning the first three games in a series (8)

13 "Naked Maja" painter (4)

15 Played in goal for Detroit between 1963-70 (7)

46

17 Red Wings' home rink in the '60s (7)

20 Was both head coach and general manager for much of the 1960s (4)

22 Glue (8)

25 Type of vinegar (8)

27 Scored his first NHL goal and led the team in penalty minutes during the 1965-66 season (6)

28 Very hard (physically) (9)

29 Aquatic mammal (5)

Down

1 AKA drywall (9)

2 Used to describe something overly sentimental (8)

3 Blinded during a 1966 game against Chicago when hit in the eye, this player had to retire but went on to coach the Red Wings. (7)

4 Animal shelter (4)

5 Hall of Fame Red Wing who was ranked 99 on the *Hockey News'* 100 Greatest Hockey Players (6)

6 Led the team in penalty minutes during the '62-'63 season, with 273 (5)

9 Cinch (4)

13 "For Me and My ___" (3)

14 Two hued (9)

16 Moray, e.g. (3)

18 Speak in error (8)

19 Had 25 wins in goal during the 1963-64 season (7)

21 Was in goal for Detroit on and off throughout much of the 1960s (6)

23 Scored his 20th goal for the 17th consecutive season during a February 6, 1966 game against Boston (4)

24 Caffè ___ (5)

26 Handle roughly (4)

The 1960s – How well do you know them?

1. Who were the Red Wings playing when Gordie Howe became the first NHL player to play 1000 regular-season games?

2. What year did the original Hockey Hall of Fame open?

3. Who was the first NHL player to have back-to-back 50-goal seasons in 1965-66 and 1966-67?

4. What future great Red Wing was born on December 13, 1969 in Moscow, USSR?

5. What future Chicago great scored his first NHL goal against the Red Wings on January 25, 1964?

6. Three NHL players accumulated more than 100 points during the 1968-69 season. Can you name all of them?

7. Who scored two goals in five seconds to help the Red Wings beat the Black Hawks in the semifinals in 1965?

8. Who were the two esteemed veterans who were on line with Gordie Howe during the 1968-69 and 1969-70 season?

9. There were only two different team captains for the Red Wings in the 1960s. Who were they?

10. What three Red Wings won the Lester Patrick Award in the 1960s?

11. Who won the Calder Trophy for the 1964-65 season?

12. How many times did Gordie Howe win the Art Ross Trophy?

Solutions on page 122.

49

Legendary Red Wings: The 1960s

Solutions on page 122.

Across

1 Handle roughly (4)

3 Hack (4)

6 This Red Wing was called "Wild Thing," Howie _____. (5)

10 PC "brain" (3)

11 Camel, e.g. (9)

12 Clean, as a spill (3,2)

13 Found in church names, i.e. _____ of Sorrow (3,4)

16 He was in net for the Red Wings from 1963-70. (7)

18 Pinnacle (4)

20 This defenseman played for the Wings from 1961-66 and was head coach from 1968-70. (6)

22 "Sesame Street" watcher (3)

25 Elmer, to Bugs (3)

26 This Red Wing led the league in goals for the 1964-65 season, with 42. (6)

28 "I had no ___!" (4)

29 This Red Wing (who later went on to be their coach) was blinded in his right eye during a game in 1966 against Chicago: Doug _____. (7)

30 Red Wings goalie who followed 16 Across. (7)

33 Stake (5)

35 This left wing was known as "The Big M." (9)

36 ___ *Today* (3)

37 Any "Seinfeld," now (5)

38 "Good going!" (4)

39 Balance sheet item (4)

Down

1 Played center on a line with Gordie Howe and Alex Delvecchio in the 1960s. (9)

2 This player was nicknamed "Iron Man": Garry _____. (5)

4 Like craft shows (5)

5 "Rocks" (3)

6 "Tasty!" (3)

7 One way to buy furniture (9)

8 Rubbernecker (5)

9 Shamu, for one (4)

14 Deception (3)

15 Follow (3)

16 ___ del Sol (5)

17 Black stone (4)

19 Played on the "HUM" line with Henderson and Ullman (9)

21 Back street (5)

23 The end (5,4)

24 Lackluster (4)

27 Affirmative action (3)

28 Bank offering, for short (3)

29 Shady spot (5)

30 Set of principles (5)

31 Surfing need (4)

32 Bring up (5)

34 Seek a seat (3)

35 "Gee whiz!" (3)

Red Wings You Should Know: Alex Delvecchio

For 22 years, Alex "Fats" Delvecchio was a member of the Detroit Red Wings. He is only surpassed by Nicklas Lidstrom and Gordie Howe for playing the most games with the Red Wings. Known for his sportsmanship, he was a three-time winner of the Lady Byng trophy for combining skill with gentlemanly conduct.

While a Red Wing, Delvecchio won three Stanley Cups and served as the team captain for 12 years. He retired from playing in 1973 and went on to spend two seasons as Red Wings head coach. He was inducted into the Hockey Hall of Fame in 1977. His number, 10, was retired by the team on November 10, 1991. He is an active member of the Detroit Red Wings Alumni Association and works to raise money for a variety of causes in Michigan and Ontario.

6

The 1970s

The 1960s might have been bad, but the 1970s were worse. Between 1968 and 1982, the Red Wings had 14 head coaches. None lasted more than three seasons, many less. In their first 42 years of existence, the Red Wings had only had six coaches. The first coach of the '70s, Ned Harkness, had been a successful college coach, but his rules and style of play were not accepted by team veterans. It seems the vets didn't appreciate rules about not smoking and short haircuts. He resigned in 1973 and so ended Detroit's "Darkness with Harkness."

There were other factors contributing to the difficult decade as well. The old development system ended, so the coaches were unable to groom young players and commit them to the team at an early age. Howe retired from the team after the 1970-71 season. Frank Mahovlich was traded to Montreal after being with Detroit for just two seasons.

Bright spots like Mickey Redmond having two 50-goal seasons and the beginning of Marcel Dionne's career could not make up for a lack of goaltending and good defensive play. The Red Wings became known as "the Dead Wings."

During the 1979-80 season, the team moved into a new home: the Joe Louis Arena. Everyone was hopeful that the new ice and the new decade would mark a rebirth for the team.

Red Wings Sudoku

Use logic to fill in the boxes so each row, column and 2x4 box contain the letters R-E-D-W-I-N-G-S to celebrate the team. The top puzzle is easier than the bottom. See how you do! Solutions on page 123.

			W			E	R
		N					D
					G		
N	S					I	
	G			I	S		
		D				R	
				W			E
I			S	E			

					D		W
		W				I	
	N			S		R	
E							D
	R				N	D	E
N							
					R	G	
	S	D	G				

Number 9

Jersey 9 was retired on March 12, 1972 in honor of Gordie Howe. But he wasn't the only Red Wing to ever wear the number. Solutions on page 124.

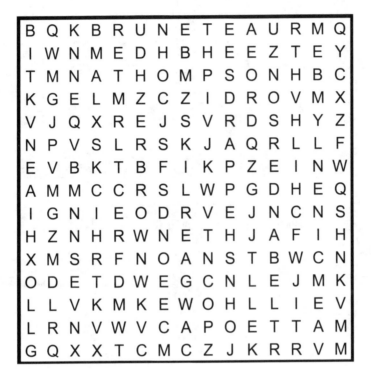

```
B  Q  K  B  R  U  N  E  T  E  A  U  R  M  Q
I  W  N  M  E  D  H  B  H  E  E  Z  T  E  Y
T  M  N  A  T  H  O  M  P  S  O  N  H  B  C
K  G  E  L  M  Z  C  Z  I  D  R  O  V  M  X
V  J  Q  X  R  E  J  S  V  R  D  S  H  Y  Z
N  P  V  S  L  R  S  K  J  A  Q  R  L  L  F
E  V  B  K  T  B  F  I  K  P  Z  E  I  N  W
A  M  M  C  C  R  S  L  W  P  G  D  H  E  Q
I  G  N  I  E  O  D  R  V  E  J  N  C  N  S
H  Z  N  H  R  W  N  E  T  H  J  A  F  I  H
X  M  S  R  F  N  O  A  N  S  T  B  W  C  N
O  D  E  T  D  W  E  G  C  N  L  E  J  M  K
L  L  V  K  M  K  E  W  O  H  L  L  I  E  V
L  R  N  V  W  V  C  A  P  O  E  T  T  A  M
G  Q  X  X  T  C  M  C  Z  J  K  R  R  V  M
```

ABEL	KILREA
ANDERSON	LAMB
BROWN	LEWIS
BRUNETEAU	MATTE
CONACHER	MCINENLY
HICKS	SHERF
HOWE	SORRELL
JOHN SHEPPARD	THOMPSON
KELLT	WISEMAN

The 1970s

Solutions on page 124.

Across

1 "___ here" (4)

3 All excited (4)

6 Accused's need (5)

10 Bidding war (7)

11 Georgia neighbor (7)

12 Voyage (7)

13 Calamitous (6)

15 Adorable one (5)

16 This center had two seasons with 20+ goals during his tenure with the Red Wings in the 1970s. (9)

18 This former Red Wing was awarded the Lester Patrick Award in 1975. (9)

21 Won the Jack Adams Award for NHL Coach of the Year in 1978 (5)

23 Received the Lester Patrick Award in 1972: James D. _____. (6)

25 Molded, as metal (3,4)

27 Paper folding (7)

28 This right wing had two 50+ goal-scoring seasons in the 1970s. (7)

30 Access the Web (3,2)

31 Attention (4)

32 Fourteen Red Wings in history have been awarded this trophy for gentlemanly play (4)

Down

1 Caribbean, e.g. (3)

2 This number-one draft pick was a solid player with the Wings from 1977-1982. (7)

4 Sack type (5)

5 Scored 50 goals during the 1974-75 season (5)

6 The books of Ezra and Daniel are written in this language (7)

7 Romance language (7)

8 Won the Lester Patrick Award in 1975 (4)

9 Lady Byng winner for the 1974-75 season (6)

12 Anubis has the head of this animal (6)

14 Head protector (6)

16 ___ juice (milk) (3)

17 Bar order (3)

19 Place for securing a boat (7)

20 Countryside (7)

21 Presses, folds and stretches (6)

22 The art of public speaking (7)

24 Played in goal 43 times for the Red Wings during the 1971-72 season (5)

25 Dreary sound (5)

26 Edible bird (4)

29 Tail (3)

The 1970s – How well do you know them?

1. What record was set by Gordie Howe in October 1971?

2. Marcel Dionne broke the NHL record for points for a rookie in 1972, with 75 points. Who did he surpass?

3. Who did the Red Wings acquire with their first overall pick in the 1977 draft?

4. What two new franchises were added to the NHL for the 1970-71 season?

5. What division were the two new teams in?

6. What league began competing against the NHL during the 1972-73 season?

7. How many teams were there? Can you name them?

8. What two new teams were added to the NHL for the '72-'73 season?

9. How many goals did Gordie Howe score at age 45 when playing for the Houston Aeros with sons Marty and Mark?

10. Which NHL team finished the 1976-77 regular season with just one at-home loss?

11. How long had it been since the Red Wings made the playoffs when Bobby Kromm had his Jack Adams Award-winning season with the team in 1977-78?

12. Who was awarded the Art Ross Trophy during the 1979-80 season, narrowly beating out Wayne Gretzky by just two goals?

Solutions on page 125.

Name That Red Wing

Can you name the 1970s Red Wing with only three clues? Solutions on page 125.

1. I was born in Stratford, Ontario in 1945.

   I was a left winger.

   I was the Red Wings' captain for two seasons, 1973 and 1979.

2. I was a Red Wing for four seasons.

   I was a center.

   I have been head coach at my alma mater for more than 20 years.

3. I won two Stanley Cups while playing with the Montreal Canadiens.

   I was the first Red Wing to score 50 goals in a season.

   I am a color analyst for Fox Sports Detroit.

4. I was born in 1951 in Drummondville, Centre-du-Quebec.

   I played 18 seasons in the NHL for Detroit, Los Angeles and New York.

   I was inducted into the Hockey Hall of Fame in 1992.

5. My middle name is Gunnar.

   I was co-winner of the Charlie Conacher Humanitarian Award in 1973.

   I was traded in 1973 to the Minnesota North Stars for Ted Harris.

6. I was the 10th overall pick in the 1969 NHL draft.

   I played for four teams during my 15 years in the NHL.

   I am a part-owner of the Carolina Hurricanes.

7. I was born in Saskatchewan in 1953.

   I was known as "Polo."

   I set the club record with eight penalties during a game on March 24, 1976.

8. I was the first pick in the 1977 NHL draft.

   I played professional hockey from 1977-1991.

   I finished my playing career with the HC Ambri-Piotta in Switzerland, who retired my jersey.

9. I was born in Hodonin, Czechoslovakia.

   I played five seasons with Detroit.

   I am currently the manager of the Slovak national team in North America.

10. I was a Golden Gopher.

    I scored the most points for a rookie defenseman during the 1977-78 season.

    I was elected to the United States Hockey Hall of Fame in 1996.

Red Wings You Should Know: Mickey Redmond

Among the few bright spots during the 1970s were Mickey Redmond's two 50+ goal-scoring seasons. He started his time in the NHL with the Montreal Canadiens from 1967-71. He was traded to the Wings in 1971 in exchange for Frank Mahovlich.

During the '72-'73 season, he surpassed Gordie Howe's record of 49 Red Wing goals in a season with 52 goals and 93 points. Redmond's record would stand until 1985, when John Ogrodnick scored 55.

While playing with the Wings, Redmond was on lines with hockey greats like Alex Delvecchio and Marcel Dionne. Today, Redmond is a color commentator for Red Wings games on Fox Sports Detroit.

7
The 1980s

In 1982 the Norris family sold the Red Wings to Mike and Marion Ilitch, owners of the Little Caesars pizza chain. In 1983, the Wings selected Steve Yzerman with the fourth pick in the draft ... a new arena, new ownership, new talent. Change was in the air.

Jim Devellano was brought in as general manager in '82, and the team hired veteran coach Jacques Demers. The Wings made the playoffs five seasons during the decade, and Demers was the NHL Coach of the Year for the '86-'87 and '87-'88 seasons.

By the start of the '89 season, Yzerman had been named team captain and had set team records during the previous year for goals, assists and points (65, 90 and 155, respectively). Together with his line mates, Gerard Gallant and Paul MacLean, Yzerman racked up 319 points that season, the most by any Red Wings line ever.

Also in 1989, Detroit signed three of Europe's brightest stars, Nicklas Lidstrom, Vladimir Konstantinov and Sergei Fedorov, all of whom would be important to the team's continued climb back to dominance in the 1990s.

Number 19

Jersey 19 was retired January 2, 2007 in honor of Steve Yzerman. But he wasn't the only Red Wing to ever wear the number. The following players are among the 19's that graced the roster over the years.See if you can find them in the facing grid. Solution on page 126.

ABEL	GOEGON	MACDONALD	TOPPAZINI
ALLEN	HAMEL	MARCON	VAIL
AMADIO	HARRIS	MCCARTHY	VOLMAR
BLACK	HENDERSON	MCNAB	WALL
BOLDIREV	HERCHENRATTER	MCNEILL	WATSON
CLOUTIER	HOLLINGWORTH	MULOIN	WILSON
COSTELLO	HRVMNAK	PAVELICH	WONG
DILLABOUGH	HUDSON	POILE	YZERMAN
DOAK	HULL	SALOVAARA	
DOUGLAS	JACKSON	SIMPSON	
EHMAN	KORNEY	SMITH	
FOLEY	KRULICKI	STASIUK	
FOLK	LADOUCEUR	STEMKOWSKI	
FONTEYNE	LICARI	STEWART	
GEISBRECHT	MACADAM	STRATE	

```
H W K N H G U O B A L L I D B C C
G U T O P P A Z I N I B R A L F X
N E D H N O C R A M A D A C A M S
O A I S M X P F D W K Z C C C H V
W L S S O A W T I I O V I Q K N O
H U L L B N C L I K C I L U R K L
W E C E G R S D M C N E I L L N M
H R N X T O E N O N L B M W I A A
O M E D N S E C D N I O W Z I A R
L W C T E K O G H N A O U C V Y V
L M S C T R K C O T B L L T S J J
I C T P A A S X L N E A D U I S D
N N R X O R R O W A L L H A M E L
G A A D N I T N N S T A S I U K R
W B T S A Y L H E T Q D T S D H H
O O E Y M A J E Y H R H T R O C R
R I V E H R H Z N U C E Y I U I V
T D E N E A R A E O W R Z M G L M
H A R R V A I C R A S F E U L E N
A M G O V V U W R R O P R H A V A
J A C K S O N T A L I N M K S A K
V E R I D L O B E T O S A I L P Q
M P J A A A R Y P Z S W N X S O V
N E L L A S S T E M K O W S K I F
I K A E U A D E N Y E T N O F G Z
```

The 1980s

Solutions on page 127.

Across

1 Traveling performers (6)

4 "Good grief!" (4)

7 "Go on ..." (3)

10 Court figure (5)

11 www.yahoo.com, e.g. (3)

12 Brazilian city (5)

13 Boosts (4)

14 X-man (6)

15 Neither's partner (3)

17 Talent (7)

18 Invigorating drinks (6)

21 With hands on hips (6)

23 Number 19 (7)

25 "Much ___ About Nothing" (3)

27 Bob Marley's music (6)

28 French railway stop (4)

30 Begin (3,2)

31 Common soccer score (3)

32 One of the five basic tastes: sweet, sour, bitter, salty and _____ (5)

33 Discouraging words (3)

34 "Groovy!" (4)

35 Red Wings owner since 1982 (6)

Down

1 India's number one tourist attraction (3,5)

2 Red Wing from 1979-1987, is 12th in total points for the franchise (9)

3 City greenery (4)

5 AKA as "Turkey," this Red Wing was an alternate captain for the team in the 1980s. (7)

6 Found at "coming out" parties (10)

7 ___ wrench (5)

8 Former Red Wing coach who currently serves in the Canadian Senate (6)

9 Helped lead the Wings during the '83-'84 season with 33 goals and 47 assists (6)

16 Cool it (6,4)

19 Fight participant (9)

20 Where the corn should be by July 4 (4,4)

22 Dress material (7)

23 Every twelve months (6)

24 Red Wing from 1976-1986, team captain for the '81-'82 season (6)

26 Played for the Red Wings from '85-'89, had 62 assists in the '88-'89 season (5)

29 Feed (4)

The 1980s – How well do you know them?

1. Who led the team in assists for the 1980-81 season?

2. Name the three individuals associated with the Red Wings who were given the Lester Patrick Award in the 1980s.

3. Which Red Wing was awarded the Bill Masterson Trophy for perseverance for the 1983-84 season?

4. How old was Steve Yzerman when he became team captain for the Red Wings?

5. How many years was he captain for the Red Wings?

6. Steve Yzerman scored his first goal in the NHL on October 5, 1983. Against which team was he playing?

7. Who was Detroit's number-one pick in the 1986 NHL entry draft?

8. Jacques Demers is the only NHL coach to win this prestigious award in back-to-back seasons. What is it?

9. Formerly involved in Red Wings ownership, this NHL president was the one responsible for making helmet-wearing mandatory in the league.

10. Did Steve Yzerman ever win the Hart Trophy?

11. Who holds the franchise record for most penalty minutes in a season?

Solutions on page 127.

Yzerman Sudoku

Use logic to fill in the boxes so each row, column and 2x4 box contain the letters S-Y-Z-E-R-M-A-N to celebrate famed Red Wing Steve Yzerman. Solution on page 128.

Name That Red Wing

Can you name the 1980s Red Wing with only three clues? Solutions on page 128.

1. I was drafted third overall by the Red Wings in the 1979 NHL draft.

   I played right wing.

   I was an assistant coach of the Anaheim Ducks in 2010.

2. I was born in West Germany.

   I played 10 years in the NHL.

   When I was drafted in 1978, I was the largest player in league history (6'5", 225 lbs.).

3. I won two AHL Calder Cup titles while playing for the Nova Scotia Voyageurs.

   I scored 19 goals my rookie season.

   I currently serve as a radio color analyst for the Red Wings.

4. I was a two-time All-Star while playing for the Buffalo Sabres.

   I was a Red Wing from 1981-1986.

   I was briefly an assistant coach for the Tampa Bay Lightning.

5. I was drafted 66th overall by the Red Wings in 1979.

   I was a left winger.

   I am currently the vice president of the Red Wings Alumni Association.

6. I played pee wee hockey on the same team with Wayne Gretzky.

    I was in goal for the Wings from 1982-1990.

    My name is on the Stanley Cup for being the goalie coach/scout of the 2006 Carolina Hurricanes.

7. I played on the same line as Steve Yzerman at left wing.

    I played for both Detroit and Tampa Bay.

    I am currently an assistant coach with the Montreal Canadiens.

8. I allowed the first career NHL goal scored by Wayne Gretzky.

    I was a Red Wing from 1986-1991.

    I am the head coach of the Slovak national ice hockey club.

9. I was born in Sarnia, Ontario.

    I was the seventh overall pick in the 1984 NHL draft.

    I totaled 1069 penalty minutes during my 16 seasons in the NHL with three different teams.

10. I scored 62 goals during the 1992-93 season.

    I scored my last goal as a Carolina Hurricane during the 1999 Stanley Cup playoffs.

    My number 3 was not officially retired by the Hurricanes, but no one has worn it since my death in 1999.

Red Wings You Should Know: Steve Yzerman

"The Captain" dressed as captain of the Red Wings for more than 1300 games, making him the longest-serving captain of any professional sport in North America. He led the Red Wings to five first-place NHL seasons and three Stanley Cup championships (1997, 1998 and 2002). He also was a 10-time NHL All-Star.

His 20+ years in a Red Wing uniform also led to a lot of hardware. Yzerman won the 1989 Lester B. Pearson Award, the 1998 Conn Smythe Trophy, the 2000 Selke Trophy and the Bill Masterson Memorial Trophy in 2003. His #19 Red Wings jersey was retired in 2007, and he was inducted into the Hockey Hall of Fame in 2009.

Yzerman spent many years in the Red Wings front office before accepting a job as general manager for the Tampa Bay Lightning in 2010.

8

The 1990s

The decade did not begin auspiciously–the Red Wings missed the playoffs after the 1989-90 season, and consequently Coach Demers found his services were no longer required by the team. He was replaced by Bryan Murray, the former Washington Capital's coach, who helped bring the team's offense to the top of the NHL.

Many great young players like Slava Kozlov, Keith Primeau, Martin Lapointe, Darren McCarty and Chris Osgood joined the Wings' roster and helped bring up the team's scoring. They were aided by the acquisition by trade of some skilled veterans, like Dino Ciccarelli, Paul Coffey and Ray Sheppard.

However, it wasn't until Scotty Bowman took the job behind the bench in 1993 that things started really coming together. Bowman's insistence that the team really work on defense paid dividends in the strike-shortened 1994-95 season. The Wings won the President's Trophy for the NHL's best season record, and Paul Coffey was the Norris Trophy winner for best defenseman. They lost in the final round of the Stanley Cup playoffs to the New Jersey Devils, but it was clear that they were contenders again.

The following season saw the team win 62 games, an NHL record for most wins in a season. Bowman collected the Jack Adams Award, Osgood and Vernon shared the Jennings Trophy, and Fedorov took home the Selke Trophy. Unfortunately the Wings were defeated in the Western Conference Finals by the eventual Stanley Cup-winning Colorado Avalanche.

During the offseason, the Red Wings acquired Brendan Shanahan, who proved to be the final puzzle piece needed to bring home the 1997 Stanley Cup–Detroit's first in more than 40 years.

With the good, however, there is always the bad. The Wings family was shocked just a few days after the playoffs when star defenseman Vladimir Konstantinov was critically injured in an automobile accident, forcing him to retire from the game.

However, Konstantinov was present for the Stanley Cup Finals the next year when the Red Wings beat out the Washington Capitals and was able to raise the cup from his wheelchair on the ice.

Number 16

Anderson	Francis	Konstantinov	Seiling
Bergeron	Gage	Laforge	Smith
Boucha	Gallagher	MacGregor	Starr
Bowman	Glover	Mackay	Stewart
Boyd	Goldsworthy	Marker	St. Laurent
Brown	Hampson	McFadden	Ullman
Chabot	Hanson	McIntyre	Unger
Cloutier	Harris	Moffatt	Voss
Couture	Hicks	Orlando	Wall
Diachuk	Jennings	Quackenbush	Webster
Doran	Jones	Rossignol	Wilson
Douglas	Kirton	Roulston	Wochy
Fisher	Kisio	Sclisizzi	

Number 16

Although not officially retired by the Red Wings, the number 16 has not been worn by anyone since Vladimir Konstantinov. However, there were lots of Wings who wore the number before. Some are listed in the puzzle below. How many can you find? Players hidden in the puzzle are listed on the facing page. Solution is on page 129.

The 1990s

Solutions on page 129.

Across

8 Swain (4)

9 Uniform shade (5)

10 Air (4)

11 Tied record for most shorthanded goals scored by a defenseman in the playoffs in the 1997-98 run for the Cup (6)

13 He writes the songs. (8)

14 The Hartford Whalers traded him to Detroit for Keith Primeau, Paul Coffey and a first-round pick in the 1997 draft. (8)

18 Modern phone feature (6)

21 The first player to win an Olympic silver medal in hockey and a Stanley Cup in the same year (1998) (7)

23 Scored his 500th goal during the 1995-96 season (7)

27 Three-time Stanley Cup-winning coach of the Red Wings (6)

30 Seven-time Norris Trophy winner from Sweden (8)

32 Fortunately, his cancer was _____. (8)

34 Winner of the Norris Trophy for the 1994-95 season (6)

37 "Guilty," e.g. (4)

38 Atlanta-based airline (5)

39 Fedorov, Kozlov, Konstantinov, Fetisov and Larionov were known as the "Russian ____" (4)

Down

1 Children's ___ (4)

2 Things that go ____ in the night. (4)

3 "Fine by me" (4)

4 Romeo and Juliet hang out (7)

5 Mood lighting necessity (6)

6 Shared the Jennings Trophy with Mike Vernon for the 1995-96 season (6)

7 Red Wing in the 1990s for three seasons: Mark ____ (4)

12 Recreational hockey league for adults (3)

15 Go quickly (3,2)

16 *The Matrix* hero (3)

17 "Deadwood" airer (3)

19 Dolly, for one (3)

20 "Remember the ___!" (5)

22 Genetic letters (3)

24 "Kneel before ___!" (3)

25 Backstabber (3)

26 Older (7)

28 Former Red Wing coach that is currently GM of the Ottawa Senators (6)

29 Not a single soul (6)

31 BART stop (3)

33 ___ *Fiction* (4)

34 Kind of court (4)

35 Often played by men wearing tricornered caps (4)

36 A deadly sin (4)

The 1990s – How well do you know them?

1. Which three Red Wings made the NHL All-Rookie team in the 1990s?

2. Name the two Red Wings who won the NHL Plus/Minus Award in the 1990s.

3. Vladimir Konstantinov was injured when the limo he had hired to drive him home from a Stanley Cup victory party crashed into a tree. Who else was in the car with him?

4. What did the special patch worn by the Wings during the 1997-98 season say on it?

5. What was the name of the system that Scotty Bowman and assistant coaches Barry Smith and Dave Lewis implemented to improve Red Wing defense?

6. What happened to Mike Vernon after winning the Conn Smythe Trophy in 1997?

7. Who won the Conn Smythe Trophy in 1998?

8. Who did Paul Coffey pass to become the highest-scoring defenseman in NHL playoff history?

9. Scotty Bowman's 1000th career victory came against what NHL team?

Solutions on page 130.

Stanley Cup Sudoku

Use logic to fill in the boxes so each row, column and 2x5 box contain the letters S-T-A-N-L-E-Y-C-U-P to celebrate sports' ultimate prize. Solution on page 130.

			C		N				S
			P	L	E		Y	T	
L	N				Y		E		
			A	E					P
			L			S	N		C
								E	
					A				
		U	T				C		Y
	T		Y	A				P	
N	C							S	A

Missing Wings

Using the clue below, identify and then find the correct Red Wing in the word search on page 81. Solutions onn page 131.

1. Dressed as captain for over 1300 games

2. Sometimes called "Vlad the Impaler"

   _____

3. This Russian was traded to Buffalo in 2001 for Dominik Hasek.

   _____

4. Supposedly married Anna Kournikova in 2001

   _____

5. Won the 1997 Conn Smyth Trophy

   _____

6. Is one of only five NHL goalies to have scored by shooting the puck directly into the opponent's net

   _____

7. Scored the cup-clinching goal in game four of the Stanley Cup playoffs in 1997.

   _____

8. Sometimes called "The Professor"

   _____

9. Was on four Stanley Cup-winning teams in the 1990s, the only NHLer to do so

   _____

10. Is currently the NHL vice president of hockey and business development

    _____

11. Won seven James Norris Memorial Trophies.

    _____

```
D E L Q D M N R G G T M T K V
O V L M Z G I J M T E P D R O
F O H I F H X K Y E N S N K N
B R Y P Q H S T E C T A N M I
R O N G X W S H X V M Z E Y T
E D N A W A Y E M R E V T R N
N E W A M H R B E Y O R T Y A
D F B X H C N Z Y L A D N V T
A I W H U T Y F Z C X O N O S
N E Q X K E D O C Z T O I H N
S G Y B V G K M J M O G C O O
H R Y E P A N I J V Y S K B K
A E T T V E W G V H U O L U R
N S E A R T W O P P P S A Y I
A X L R U W C R S S X I S Z M
H S A N R Z U L G V C R L U I
A D P M C M Y A F G K H I D D
N N K Q Y H O R X Z F C D I A
X C Q R L C U I A I Z J S A L
B R R C T X P O P Z K R T W V
K A I T J D I N T G G N R Q T
L D W V P P L O P C P Y O N K
L R H L D I F V F F E E M F H
```

Red Wings You Should Know: Sergei Fedorov

In 1990, while playing with the CSKA Moscow team at the Goodwill Games in Seattle, Sergei Fedorov sneaked out of his hotel room and onto a plane for Detroit, defecting from the Soviet Union for a career in the NHL. Described by no less than Steve Yzerman as "the best skater I've ever seen," Fedorov was the recipient of both the Golden Hart Memorial Trophy (MVP) and the Lester B. Pearson Award (most outstanding player).

He played as a Red Wing from the 1990-91 season until 2002-2003, helping lead the team to three Stanley Cup championships.

Fedorov left the NHL in 2009 to be captain of the Metallurg Magnitogorsk team in the Kontinental Hockey League and play with his brother Fedor. It was their father's lifelong dream that his two sons would play together.

9
The 2000s

Welcome to a new millenium! The acquisitions of Chris Chelios and Pat Verbeek helped the Red Wings continue to be dominant in 1999-2000, as longtime stars like Yzerman continued to rack up milestones like 600 goals and 1500 points. Other impressive targets hit that season included Verbeek achieving 500 goals and 1000 points, Shanahan getting 400 goals and Fedorov moving past the 300 goals mark. Yzerman won the Selke Trophy at season's end and was selected to be an All-Star along with Brendan Shanahan and Nicklas Lidstrom.

In 2001, the Wings were eliminated in the first round of the playoffs despite having the second-best record that season. Lidstrom was awarded for his efforts with his first Norris Trophy. To help elevate the team's play, more talent was brought in that summer: Dominik Hasek, Brett Hull and Luc Robitaille helped the Red Wings go the distance. The Red Wings were Stanley Cup champions again in 2002, after finishing the season with a league's best 116 points. Lidstrom won his second Norris Trophy for his defensive work in 2002, but he was also the recipient of the Conn Smythe Trophy for playoff MVP.

Scotty Bowman retired after the season, and although the Red Wings had a few years of great seasonal play (with a brief break for the 2004-2005 lockout), they posted disappointing results in the playoffs. For the 2007-2008 season, all the stars seemed to realign, and the team finished the regular season with 54 wins, their third over-50 finish in three seasons. They went on to be a dominant presence in the playoffs and eventually beat the Pittsburgh Penguins to secure their 11th Stanley Cup Championship.

In addition to the Stanley Cup, the team won the Presidents' Trophy and the Clarence Campbell Bowl. Henrik Zetterburg was awarded the Conn Smythe Trophy for playoff MVP.

The NHL Awards Night that year was a massive celebration of Red Wings. Pavel Datsyuk was awarded the Selke Trophy and the Lady Byng Trophy. Nicklas Lidstrom was awarded his sixth Norris Trophy, and Chris Osgood and Dominik Hasek shared the Jennings Trophy. To cap off the night, Gordie Howe was given the NHL Lifetime Achievement Award.

Trophy Winners in the 2000s

Lady Byng Trophy
Pavel **Datsyuk** (2005-06, 2006-07, 2007-08, 2008-09)

Norris Trophy
Nicklas **Lidstrom** (2000-01, 2001-02, 2002-03, 2005-06, 2006-07, 2007-08, 2010-2011)

Selke Trophy
Kris **Draper** (2003-04)
Pavel **Datsyuk** (2007-08, 2008-09)

Plus- Minus Award
Chris **Chelios** (2001-02)

Bill Masterson Trophy
Steve **Yzerman** (2002-03)

Conn Smythe Trophy
Nicklas **Lidstrom** (2002)
Henrik **Zetterberg** (2008)

William M. Jennings Trophy
Dominik **Hasek** and Chris **Osgood** (2007-08)

King Clancy Award
Brendan **Shanahan** (2002-2003)

Mark Messier Leadership Award
Chris **Chelios** (2007-08)

NHL Lifetime Achievement Award
Gordie **Howe** (2008)

Trophy Winners in the 2000s

Can you find the Red Wings and the hardware they accumulated during the first 10 years of the 2000s? We've highlighted the words to look for in the word list. Solution on page 132.

```
O X M Y C Q N S D M E L Q B E C M
D R A H D B H C O L R C Q H L A C
D W P F F A C P A C E T C R N N K
B A K Y N B B G O G P O F W H O Y
Y C N A L C G N I K A P F X L R P
D S H A A J N R N O R R I S L A P
K A O J H S Q I E E D R S T I T I
N E E I M V F H I B B N I K F H B
O H X Y L Z A S I I R Z U C E Z X
S S T L E E S S T L F E Y Z T Q F
R H G K W E H G S M O I T T I H X
E K L O M B N C V R P S S T M O M
T E H K O Y T U E X L P Q S E Y W
S S R H B D A T S Y U K G F A Z I
A A D Y E Z N E P F S H H G C E O
M H D C O S A A F I M K X P H R L
L A R A E X L E N M I K I V I M Z
L I D S T R O M V O N K B E E A L
I G C G N I G S B H U G N M V N K
B U M N Q V S U L B S X I P E P Z
R G S I L Y M V D F S G T T M B U
S G C N I S L I L C I E L D E O D
K H R N P T J O G H K T J W N J E
Y F Q E W G H R Z J W X I D T V Q
N E L J T S X N G J C P I T W U X
```

The 2000s

Solutions on page 132.

Across

3 Sot's sound (3)

8 Caviar source (6)

9 Boston hockey legend (3)

10 2002 Winter Olympics locale (4)

11 Amscrayed (3)

12 Propel, in a way (3)

13 Lens cover? (6)

15 Bout enders, for short (3)

16 Dash (4)

17 Ascap alternative (3)

18 Imagination (10)

21 Shopping ___ (4)

23 Sad event for hockey fans in 2004-05 (7)

25 Scored six game-winning goals during the 2007-08 campaign to break Gordie Howe's franchise record (7)

29 Six-time Norris Trophy winner (8)

32 Baker's offering (6)

35 Labyrinth (4)

36 Chelios was acquired from this NHL team. (10)

40 Debtor's note (3)

41 Awarded to Shanahan for the program he started that purchases and installs smoke detectors for low-income households: ____ Clancy Memorial Trophy (4)

42 Speedometer letters (3)

43 Team that Pat Verbeek played for before Detroit (6)

44 Cool (3)

45 From January until now (3)

Down

1 Stand up to (4)

2 Recorded his 700th goal during the 2001-02 season, to become the sixth player in

NHL history to reach that mark (4)

3 Spirits (4,6)

4 Hasek replacement in 2008 (7)

5 Penguin star (6)

6 Defeated by the Red Wings in the 2002 Stanley Cup Championship (10)

7 Word with belly or tap (6)

13 "Yadda, yadda, yadda" (3)

14 *The Three Faces of* ___ (3)

19 *Flying Down to* ___ (3)

20 "Don't ___!" (3)

22 *The Joy Luck Club* author (3)

23 Joke response (3)

24 Bounder (3)

26 Bad-mouth (3)

27 Corn serving (3)

28 Understanding (7)

30 Emphatic, in a way (6)

31 Santa's means of transportation (6)

33 ___ Wednesday (3)

34 Haul (3)

36 Contusion (4)

37 Captain ___ (4)

38 ___-bodied (4)

39 Top Tatar (4)

The 2000s – How well do you know them?

1. According to *The Hockey News*, what Red Wing has 17 "Gordie Howe Hat Tricks" (a goal, an assist and a fight) — 15 more than Gordie Howe?

2. Who was the team leader for goals in the 2000-2001 season?

3. Why was there no All-Star game in 2002?

4. Name the four teams that Detroit had to beat in the Stanley Cup playoffs to be champions in 2002.

5. Who came back from retirement for the 2003-2004 season?

6. How many Red Wings represented Sweden in the 2006 Turin Olympics?

7. Who came back to play for the Red Wings in goal during the 2006-2007 season?

8. Which coach was behind the bench for the 2008 Stanley Cup playoffs?

9. Seven former Red Wings received the Lester Patrick Award in the first 10 years of the new millenium. Can you name them?

10. How many games did Steve Yzerman play in a Red Wings uniform?

Solutions on page 133.

"The Dominator" Sudoku

Use logic to fill in the boxes so each row, column and 2x3 box contain the letters D-H-A-S-E-K to celebrate Czech goaltending sensation Dominik Hasek. Solution on page 133.

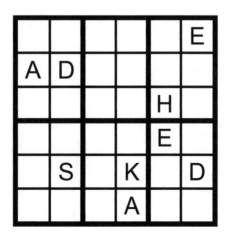

No Time Like the Present

Solutions on page 134.

Across

3 Cockeyed (5)

6 "Far out!" (7)

7 In doubt (4)

9 Black gold (3)

10 Breed (4)

11 Check for fit (3,2)

12 Comparative word (4)

13 It may be stroked. (3)

14 Warm, so to speak (4)

15 Durable wood (3)

17 Skiier Raich's home town (4)

18 Big pooch (3)

19 Advantage (4)

21 Hackneyed (5)

22 Contradict (4)

23 Morgue, for one (3)

24 Alone (4)

90

25 Sue Grafton's ___ *for Lawless* (3)

27 Bawdy (4)

29 Moo goo gai pan pan (3)

30 Mass number (4)

32 "I give up!" (5)

34 Bone dry (4)

35 Cutting tool (3)

36 Religious image: Var. (4)

37 Bette Midler instrument (7)

38 Cathedral topper (5)

Down

1 2008's Conn Smythe winner (10)

2 First Nunavut player in the NHL (6)

3 Ethereal (4)

4 Known for his back-pedaling boarding hits (8)

5 Weaken (4)

6 Building block (5)

8 Called "The Mule" by Steve Yzerman (7)

16 Hails from Sumperk, Czechoslovakia (5)

17 Played college hockey for Michigan State University (10)

20 Ron Francis is the only other player beside him to have won both the Selke and Lady Byng trophies. (7)

21 Appeared in his 1000th NHL game in 2010 (8)

26 Home country of goalie Jonas Gustavsson (6)

28 Scored his first goal as a Red Wing on October 7, 2011. (5)

31 Belonging to Bert's twin (4)

33 Game name (4)

Red Wings You Should Know: Pavel Datsyuk

Alternate captain Pavel Datsyuk won the Frank J. Selke Trophy for three consecutive seasons (2007-08 through 2009-10) and four consecutive Lady Byng Trophies. He and Ron Francis (Pittsburgh) are the only players to have been awarded both the Selke and Lady Byng trophies during their careers.

Datsyuk was born in Sverdlovsk, Russia, and was considered by many to be too small for hockey. He, however, came into his own when Vladimir Krikunov, a noted Olympic trainer, began coaching HC Dynamo Moscow. Datsyuk was noticed by the Red Wings scout prior to the draft of 1998, and the rest is history!

10

Team Owners

The Red Wings have only been owned by two families: the Norris family and the Ilitch family. Both families have been very committed to the Red Wings and keeping players, former players and fans together.

James E. Norris

James E. Norris' family had become wealthy in the 19th century, owning mills and a fleet of ships, in addition to a great deal of land. When Norris was 18, his father moved their company headquarters from Canada to Chicago. Norris became president of Norris Grain at the age of 28, and by the 1930s, his company was the largest cash grain buyer in the world. In 1932, after years of attempting to start, buy or reorganize other hockey franchises, the NHL approved Norris' bid to buy the Detriot Falcons. He also contrived to be a major player in the Chicago Black Hawks (partial owner of the team and landlord), the largest shareholder in Madison Square Garden as well as a minority shareholder in the New York Rangers. His love of hockey held through his death on December 4, 1952, and he was inducted into the Hockey Hall of Fame in 1958.

Bruce and Marguerite Norris

Upon James E. Norris' death, the team was left to two of his children, Bruce and Marguerite. Marguerite was named president and was the first woman to be engraved on the Stanley Cup in 1954 and 1955. After winning the Cup in '55, Bruce bought his sister out and became sole owner of the franchise. He was inducted into the Hockey Hall of Fame in 1969 and was awarded the Lester Patrick Trophy in 1976 for outstanding service to hockey in the United States. In 1982, Bruce decided to sell the team, and after 50 years in the Norris family, ownership went in a new direction.

Michael Ilitch

A first-generation American, Mike Ilitch is an entrepreneur, founder and owner of the pizza franchise Little Caesars. He and his wife serve as chairman and vice chairwoman of Ilitch Holdings. After purchasing the Red Wings in 1982 and leading them back to success, Ilitch went on to purchase the Detroit Tigers of the MLB in 1992 (funnily enough from another pizza magnate, Tom Monaghan of Domino's Pizza). He expressed interest in buying the Detroit Pistons in 2010 but did not pursue the venture. Ilitch was inducted into the Hockey Hall of Fame in 2003.

How well do you know Mike Ilitch?

1. Where did Mike Ilitch attend high school?

2. Of which branch of the military was he a member?

3. What position did he play for the Tiger's minor league ball club?

4. What was the name of Mike and Marian Ilitch's first pizza restaurant?

5. How many children do the Ilitchs' have?

6. The Ilitchs' commitment to reviving downtown Detroit includes purchasing this city landmark and renovating it.

Solutions on page 134.

Red Wings' Stanley Cup Winning Years

Find and circle the winning years. Answers on page 135.

```
1 1 1 9 9 8 8 2 4
1 9 9 9 1 5 0 5 4
2 5 3 5 9 9 3 0 7
3 5 6 4 2 7 5 5 2
9 1 8 3 9 4 4 0 2
4 0 4 5 9 1 0 5 2
7 0 9 8 8 2 9 7 7
5 0 8 1 3 5 4 3 8
8 8 4 6 2 1 8 5 7
```

1936	1950	1955	2002
1937	1952	1997	2008
1943	1954	1998	

MY Team (Literally)

Solutions on page 135.

Across

4 "And I Love ___" (3)

6 Displace (7)

7 "Dilbert" cartoonist Scott Adams has one: Abbr. (3)

8 Abate (3)

10 "Absolutely!" (3)

11 Owned the Red Wings from 1952-82 (5)

12 Ellington and Wellington (5)

13 Burden (3)

14 Battering device (3)

16 Impaired driving can lead to this ... (3)

17 Married to 7 Down (6)

19 College teacher (abbr.) (4)

21 African antelope (3)

22 Friends and neighbors (4)

25 Graduate (6)

26 Bit in a horse's mouth (3)

28 Chain letters? (3)

30 Toni Morrison's "___ Baby" (3)

31 Ruffle (5)

32 Thorny evergreen shrub (5)

34 "___ alive!" (3)

35 "Dig in!" (3)

36 Brown, e.g. (3)

37 Recount (7)

38 Victorian, for one (3)

Down

1 10 C-notes (4)

2 This Norris that left the Red Wings in 1952 to help run the Chicago Black Hawks. (5,1)

3 Unhappy nickname for the Red Wings bought by the Ilitches (4,5)

4 Needle holder? (8)

5 Type of free agent (10)

6 In utero (6)

7 Owner of the Red Wings, to friends (4)

9 Sport that was also of interest to 2 Down (6)

15 This Norris was the first woman to be engraved on the Stanley Cup. (10)

18 Over the top (3,2,4)

20 Disney flick (8)

23 One of the business ventures that 24 Down was involved in (6)

24 This Norris played hockey at McGill University. (5,1)

27 Other Detroit team owned by the Ilitch family (6)

29 Branch of the armed services that the Norris brothers joined (4)

33 Be itinerant (4)

North American Red Wings

The players found in the puzzle below all originate from the U.S.A. or Canada. Can you find them all? Solutions on page 136.

```
F D Y W L S P C O N N E R N S X Y O K
I R F U M T O D S M I T H R P O F H B
S A O A V N I E I R C F P M A M J U Y
M W P W K O V K R F N N O V X I V S T
B O K L P A Y E C N I U Q H V T F R V
W H I T E A X X D Z E G A X M C J C J
Q N N D W E S H Z Y O B H K T M L M N
Y R A E L C S U R K A G Y J W L H V L
B L J B E A T T N P V B W T O B S T W
N Q Y V D R N R X L A O A Q V O B T Z
P O A O E E A O M S B X H B G J N W Y
I C T B D L L P D I S P W M L A X Q P
X Y Y R I L E K A C J O K T H I P L U
V A D O E I T A A L A A H A T V W N P
Q L Q B G M G Z S D P M E F E S K W C
N T P W R G M V M L E H S F X S M A L
Q O P S C Q W E X S S R F J O R T L B
A V V X Q G B C Q Q J R H O J R Q F H
G B S M Z Q S G O Q B H Z X V N M A N
```

U.S.A.
ABDELKADER
CONKLIN
CONNER
HOWARD
JANIK
MILLER

CANADA
BERTUZZI
CLEARY
EAVES
EMMERTON
EXELBY
HELM

MACDONALD
QUINCEY
SHEAHAN
SMITH
WHITE

European Red Wings

The players found in the puzzle below all originate from overseas. Can you find them all? Solutions on page 136.

```
B  J  H  I  F  H  O  T  A  S  C  N  V  K  T  L  K
O  V  W  M  J  Q  X  S  F  O  S  Y  O  B  B  E  A
H  L  M  T  C  I  M  O  R  T  S  N  N  U  R  B  S
O  U  E  U  B  V  D  E  P  X  X  X  B  N  D  U  R
L  V  R  Y  F  I  L  P  P  U  L  A  N  M  L  W  U
M  T  I  D  K  D  N  J  S  N  Y  Q  U  I  S  T  M
S  K  C  D  U  V  O  E  A  S  K  I  N  D  L  Q  U
T  Y  S  H  B  X  S  X  N  K  R  O  N  W  A  L  L
R  Y  S  C  Z  E  S  Z  E  T  T  E  R  B  E  R  G
O  P  O  M  C  T  R  M  Z  K  U  W  P  F  N  F  B
M  T  N  Z  N  Q  E  P  N  X  U  L  P  I  J  V  E
R  P  Y  N  L  E  D  U  A  V  A  Y  D  J  D  F  R
F  Q  D  L  V  D  N  K  R  V  G  F  S  O  J  Z  O
O  Z  N  G  S  M  A  Y  F  D  H  I  T  T  K  D  T
Q  L  I  D  S  T  R  O  M  K  V  X  L  W  A  R  C
H  X  Q  G  J  O  N  Z  R  D  O  T  L  Y  R  D  T
I  M  O  F  B  M  D  C  B  G  G  I  C  H  R  B  Q
```

SWEDEN
ANDERSSON
BRUNNSTROM
ERICSSON
FRANZEN
HOLMSTROM
KRONWALL
LIDSTROM
NYQUIST
ZETTERBERG

RUSSIA
DATSYUK

FINLAND
FILPPULA

CZECH
HUDLER
KINDL

SLOVENIA
MURSAK

Hockey Films

There are some very fine films dedicated to our favorite sport. Although only one, that we know of, is about a Red Wing, we felt a salute to the hockey cinema wasn't out of line. Solutions on page 137.

Across

1 Cardinal (3)
3 All fired up (4)
7 Story of the 1980 U.S. Olympic Team (7)
9 Based on Red Wing Ted Lindsay's fight to create a player's union (3,5)
10 Holds close (4)
12 French comedy about an amateur hockey club (3,4)
13 This Jean-Claude Van Damme film takes place during a Pittsburgh Penguins game. (6,5)
19 Bored activity (5)
21 This movie is the story of Maurice Richard. (3,6)
23 Game piece (4)
24 Starring Paul Newman, this 1977 hockey film is a comedy classic. (4,4)
26 This hockey flick features performances by Rob Lowe, Patrick Swayze and Keanu Reeves. (10)
28 Stefan Kanachowski returns to his hometown to play with his brothers on an amateur team in this 2002 film. (5)

Down

2 With 5 Down, the Disney film that named an NHL team (5)
3 Drawer (6)
4 Stars John Wayne as a hockey player (4,2,3,6)
5 With 2 Down, the Disney film that named an NHL team. (6)
6 Hiding place (5)
8 Party time, maybe (3)
11 Hockey film starring Mike Myers: *The Love* _____ (4)
14 Short run (4)
15 Birth-related (5)
16 Balloon filler (3)
17 Russell Crowe hockey film: _____, *Alaska* (7)
18 It may get a licking. (5)
20 *The Walter Gretzky Story: Waking Up* _____ (5)
22 Throws out (6)
25 Real men don't eat this (6)
27 Starring "Stiffler," this 2011 hockey film tells the story of Doug Glatt, on-ice body guard. (4)

Red Wings You Should Know: Nicklas Lidstrom

Lidstrom played in many Swedish hockey clubs before being chosen by Detroit in the 1989 NHL draft. He played his first game in Detroit in 1991 and finished his first season as a runner-up for the Calder Trophy.

Over the course of his career, Lidstrom was the first European-born player to win the Conn Smythe Trophy, and he acquired seven Norris Trophies and helped lead the team to four Stanley Cup championships.

Lidstrom retired after the 2011-2012 season. His career totals include 264 goals and more than 870 assists.

11

Team Coaches

The team has boasted some of hockey's finest on the bench, and here follows a complete list of Red Wings' coaches with a few of the team's greatest profiled.

1926-1927—Art Duncan, Gordon "Duke" Keats
1927-1947— Jack Adams
1947-1954—Tommy Ivan
1954-1957—Jimmy Skinner
1957-1968—Sid Abel
1968-1969—Bill Gadsby
1969-1970—Bill Gadsby, Sid Abel
1970-1971—Ned Harkness, Doug Barkley
1971-1972—Doug Barkley, Johnny Wilson
1972-1973—Johnny Wilson
1973-1974—Alex Delvecchio, Ted Garvin
1974-1975—Alex Delvecchio
1975-1976—Alex Delvecchio, Doug Barkley
1976-1977—Alex Delvecchio, Larry Wilson
1977-1980—Bobby Kromm
1980-1981—Ted Lindsay, Wayne Maxner
1981-1982—Wayne Maxner, Billy Dea
1982-1985—Nick Polano
1985-1986—Harry Neale
1986-1990—Jacques Demers
1990-1993—Bryan Murray
1993-2002—William "Scotty" Bowman
2002-2004—Dave Lewis
2005-present—Mike Babcock

Red Wing Coaches You Should Know: Jack Adams

Ten years as a player with Toronto, Vancouver and Ottawa made him a Hall of Fame player, but it is for his 36-year association with the Red Wings as coach and general manager that most people know him. He led the team to three Stanley Cup victories as a coach. His overall coaching record— 413 wins, 390 losses and 161 ties—still qualifies him as the winningest coach in Red Wings history. Most of Adams wins happened without a contract, however; when James Norris bought the team, he tore up Adams' contract and told him he was on probation for one year. On the basis of just a handshake, Adams stuck around for 15 more years. The Jack Adams Award for most outstanding coach in the NHL was named in his honor in 1974.

Ted Lindsay

Although he was not one of the successful Detroit coaches, Lindsay is important to the franchise for a variety of reasons: He was a Hall of Fame player, a member of the famous "Production Line" with Gordie Howe and Sid Abel, and he helped lead the team to four Stanley Cups as a player. But perhaps Lindsay is most famous for what he did to get traded from the Red Wings. Lindsay was one of the founding members of the National Hockey League Players' Association, and he fought bravely for the players to unionize so that the owners had to share some of the teams' profits. The Norris family reacted badly to his lobbying and traded him to the Black Hawks. Although the players were eventually successful in forming a union, it was not without a great deal of personal struggle for those founding members. When Sid Abel came to be coach of the Red Wings many years later, he would talk Lindsay into coming back to play for the team. Lindsay went on to be coach and general manager of the team.

Scotty Bowman

Bowman won nine Stanley Cups as a head coach: five with the Montreal Canadiens, one with the Pittsburgh Penguins and three with the Detroit Red Wings. He won the Jack Adams Award twice in his career (1977 and 1996). Bowman is second on the Red Wings' all-time wins list. Unlike Adams, Bowman never played in the NHL. While playing in the minor leagues, he received a fractured skull from a slash by Jean-Guy Talbot, and Bowman turned to coaching. His lifetime coaching record—1244 wins, 574 losses and 314 ties in the regular season—is the best in league history.

Mike Babcock

The current head coach, Mike Babcock is the only coach to be included in the "Triple Gold Club" having won the Stanley Cup (2008), an Olympic gold medal (2010) and the IIHF world hockey championship title (2004). Babcock played college hockey at McGill University in Montreal, then went on to work his way through the coaching ranks before joining the bench for the Anaheim Ducks in 2002. After the NHL lockout in 2004-2005, Babcock came to the Red Wings, where he has a regular-season record of 352 wins and 154 losses.

Coaches

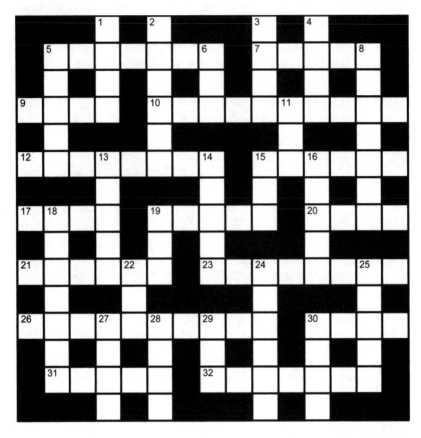

Solutions on page 137.

Across

5 Is the second-highest scoring defenseman in McGill history (7)

7 Some allege that he punched a referee in game three of the 1942 Stanley Cup Finals (5)

9 Face-to-face exam (4)

10 Served two stints as Detroit's head coach though best remembered as a player (10)

12 What goes around, comes around. (8)

15 Currently senior advisor of hockey operations for the Chicago Black Hawks. (6)

17 Biblical birthright seller (4)

19 Birds of a feather (5)

20 Advil target (4)

21 Head coach for '68-'69 (6)

23 Beastie Boys album (8)

26 Stopping point (10)

30 Won three Stanley Cups while coaching the Red Wings (1950, 1952, 1954) (4)

31 Won the 1978 Jack Adams Award (5)

32 Known in his playing days as "Terrible Ted" (7)

Down

1 His grandson is Brent Johnson, a goaltender for the Pittsburgh Penguins (4)

2 Exercise brand: ____-Trac (6)

3 Gridiron move (4)

4 Afterbath powder (4)

5 Some varieties include: straw, black and blue (5)

6 Potassium chloride (3)

8 Popeye's favorite food (7)

11 Dove's sound (3)

13 Meet me in St. ____ (5)

14 Head coach after Scotty Bowman (5)

15 Greyhound, e.g. (3)

16 Mother from "Father Knows Best": Jane ____ (5)

18 Why Susie can't sell sea shells by the sea shore: (7)

19 Wray of *King Kong* (3)

22 Dracula, at times (3)

24 Monkey chow (6)

25 Potato garnish (5)

27 "Pumping ___" (4)

28 BBs, e.g. (4)

29 Down with the flu (3)

30 M.I.T. part (abbr.) (4)

Scotty Bowman Sudoku

Use logic to fill in the boxes so each row, column and 2x3 box contain the letters B-O-W-M-A-N to celebrate one of the NHL's greatest all-time coaches. Solution on page 138.

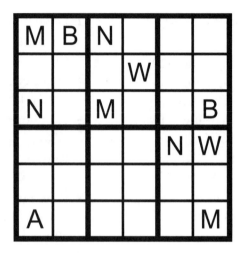

Bill Gadsby Sudoku

Use logic to fill in the boxes so each row, column and 2x3 box contain the letters G-A-D-S-B-Y to celebrate a favorite Red Wing coach and player. Solution on page 139.

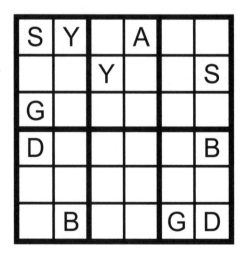

Find 'em All

Hidden in this word search are all the men who have ever coached the Detroit Red Wings. Can you find them all? Solution on page 139.

```
Y Z U S L M A R W U Y K E A T S S
W W M T I F H P X O T Q S L Q B K
O S W F F W D E M E R S E G P E I
M X L P H N E N Z H E L E A S Q N
R G B Y N F A L W N A A A D K X N
F Y I B J C W I K E R D A S Y F E
S W J U N P L R N S E B L B S P R
A C X U X S A K S D N P J Y A Y K
Z E D B O H W C B T X K K R O M M
S B Q N O J Z O T W A E S F P E H
N A L S U W K C C Y M I G Z S H N
A R E C M F M B H A P S R I U I J
K K B I C A J A B R G O A F V Q L
I L A H V I D B N R X E L R R I J
U E F Z U A T A Z U O U A A D E A
J Y Y A S D N I L M C G G G N J I
D E L V E C C H I O P V I X P O X
```

ABEL	DUNCAN	LINDSAY
ADAMS	GADSBY	MAXNER
BABCOCK	GARVIN	MURRAY
BARKLEY	HARKNESS	NEALE
BOWMAN	IVAN	POLANO
DEA	KEATS	SKINNER
DELVECCHIO	KROMM	WILSON
DEMERS	LEWIS	

Also Known As

Can you match the Red Wing with the correct nickname? Hint: Some players have more than one. Solution on page 139.

Todd Bertuzzi	Lids
Pavel Datsyuk	Ice Berg
Alex Delvecchio	Mr. Hockey
Marcel Dionne	Fats
Domink Hasek	Dominator
Gordie Howe	The Captain
Nicklas Lidstrom	The Magic Man
Ted Lindsay	Little Beaver
Henrik Zetterberg	Big Bert
Steve Yzerman	Terrible Ted
Jack Stewart	Zata
	Black Jack
	Houdini
	The Perfect Human
	Stevie Wonder

Solutions

Wilf Cude Sudoku

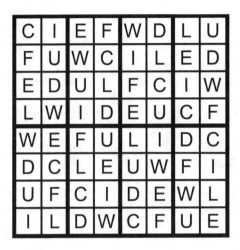

Find Some Wings

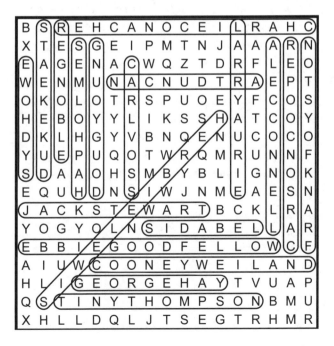

In the Beginning ...

```
A  N  T  A     S     S  L     A
K  N  O  W  A  L  L     P  A  T  R  I  C  K
I     R     C  A     A  E     O        T
M  A  R  O  O  N  S     T  O  R  O  N  T  O
B     I        K        N
O  P  S     B  L  A  D  E     A  U  R  I  E
         O        L           O     M
C  O  U  G  A  R  S     F  A  L  C  O  N  S
H     S        E        E
A  D  A  M  S     C  H  E  C  K     C  A  R
         I        U           O     A
W  I  N  D  S  O  R     R  A  C  C  O  O  N
I     O     T     E     O     H     P     G
S  O  R  R  E  L  L     P  R  O  T  E  G  E
H     M     R     Y     E     P     R     S
```

The early years: How well do you know them?

1. *Boston Bruins, Pittsburgh Pirates, Chicago Black Hawks, Detroit Cougars, New York Rangers, Ottawa Senators, Toronto St. Patricks, Montreal Maroons, Montreal Canadiens, New York Americans*

2. *1931-32 season: only one goaltender on the ice at a time; 1933-34 season: visible time clock required in every arena; 1934-35: penalty shots were instituted; 1937-38: rules governing icing put into place.*

3. *44 — the game number went up to 48 for the 1932-33 season and stayed there until 1942, when the season went up to 50 games.*

4. *Frank Fredrickson with 18 goals in the 1926-27 season, although he spent part of the year with Boston so this might count as an asterisk. The next Detroit player to be in the top 10 scorers was George Hay in 1927-1928 with 22 goals, and he was around for the whole season.*

5. *Little Dempsey, for his short (5'6") stature and offseason fitness devotion, and Little Rag Man for his ability to*

control the puck during a penalty kill

6. *No, Wings vice president Jimmy Devellano said the team refuses to hang his number because he wasn't a Hall of Famer.*

7. *Toronto Arenas, Toronto St. Pats, the Vancouver Millionaires, the Ottawa Senators. He won two Stanley Cups as a player (1918 with the TorontoArenas, 1927 with Ottawa) and was inducted into the Hockey Hall of Fame as a player in 1952.*

8. *Hay coached the minor league Detroit Olympics for three years before leaving the game entirely and going into insurance.*

9. *Border Cities Arena*

10. *The Chicago Black Hawks and Ottawa Senators*

11. *The top defenseman in the NHL. There is also a James Norris Memorial Trophy in the International Hockey League that is awarded to the top goaltender.*

Legendary Red Wings: 1926-1939

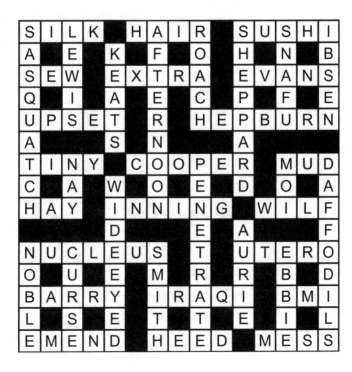

Gordie Howe Sudoku

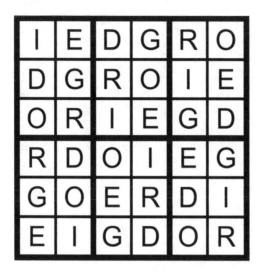

The 1943 Stanley Cup Winners

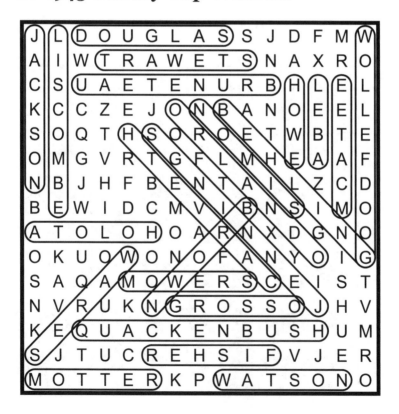

The Fabulous '40s

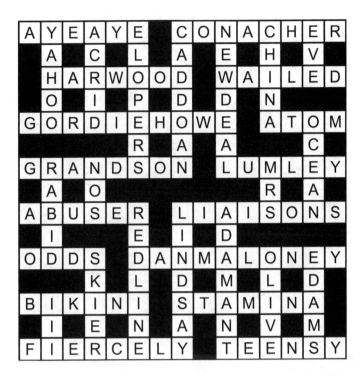

How well do you know your 1940 Red Wings?

1. *Turk Broda*
2. *Syd Howe*
3. *Detroit Red Wings, Toronto Maple Leafs and Montreal Canadiens*
4. *Ted Lindsay, Sid Abel and Gordie Howe*
5. *Frank Brimsek, also known as "Mr. Zero"*
6. *Royal Canadian Air Force*
7. *Tommy Ivan*
8. *Terry Sawchuk*
9. *Leonard "Red" Kelly*
10. *"Terrible" Ted Lindsay*
11. *A goal, an assist and a fight*
12. *Two: October 10, 1953 and March 21, 1954*

Legendary Red Wings: The 1940s

Terry Sawchuk Sudoku

The Undefeated-in-the-Playoffs '52 Stanley Cup Champions

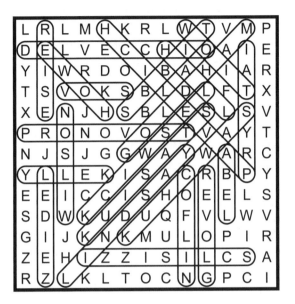

The Nifty Fifties

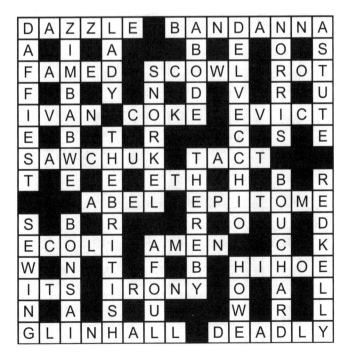

The 1950s – How well do you know them?

1. *Because the circus was booked in Madison Square Garden*
2. *Detroit traded Harry Lumley, Jack Stewart, Al Dewsbury, Don Morrison and Pete Babando for Jim Henry, Bob Goldham, Gaye Stewart and Metro Prystai. The trade was with the Chicago Black Hawks.*
3. *Zero*
4. *Sid Abel*
5. *Red Kelly*
6. *Five: 1953, 1956, 1957, 1958, 1959*
7. *It was the NHL All-Star game at Detroit's Olympia Stadium.*
8. *Johnny Wilson*
9. *Gordie Howe*
10. *The Zamboni*
11. *Elmer Lach of Montreal*
12. *Sid Abel*
13. *An octopus!*

Legendary Red Wings: The 1950s

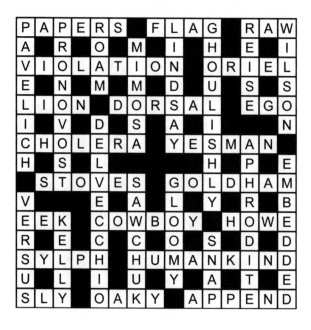

Mr. Hockey

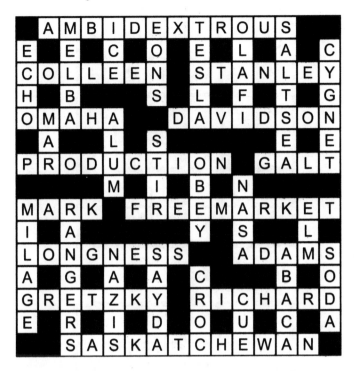

Howe about a little trivia?

1. *Toronto*

2. *Yes, two*

3. *A new car ... and as an added bonus, when Howe skated out to get it, he found his parents in the backseat. It was their first-ever NHL game.*

4. *983*

5. *Dit Clapper and Bill Gadsby*

6. *Mark Messier*

7. *Ted Kennedy (No, not the politician, the Toronto Maple Leaf.)*

Ron Murphy Sudoku

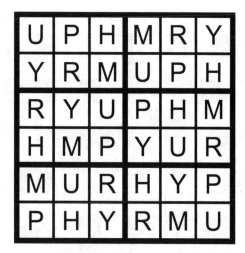

Murray Oliver Sudoku

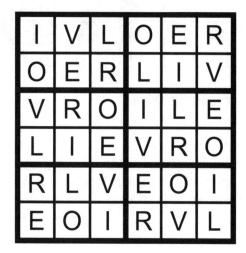

More than 20 Goals in a Season in the '60s

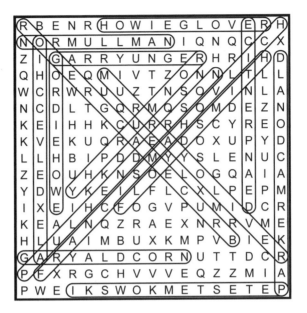

The Slightly Sad '60s

The 1960s – How well do you know them?

1. *Chicago*
2. *1961*
3. *Bobby Hull*
4. *Sergei Fedorov*
5. *Phil Esposito*
6. *Phil Esposito, Bobby Hull and Gordie Howe*
7. *Norm Ullman*
8. *Alex Delvecchio and Frank Mahovlich*
9. *Gordie Howe (1958-59 season through 1961-62 season) and Alex Delvecchio (1962-63 season through the 1972-73 season)*
10. *Gordie Howe (1967), James Norris Sr. (1967) and Jack Adams (1966)*
11. *Roger Crozier*
12. *Six, but only once during the swinging '60s.*

Legendary Red Wings: The 1960s

Red Wings Sudoku

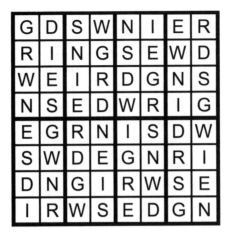

Red Wings Sudoku

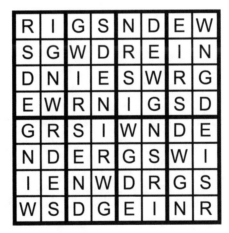

Number 9

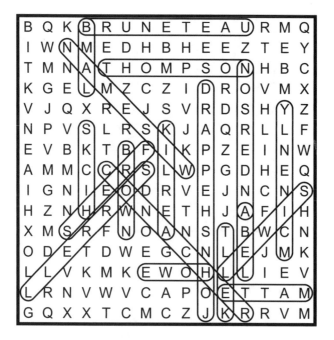

The 1970s

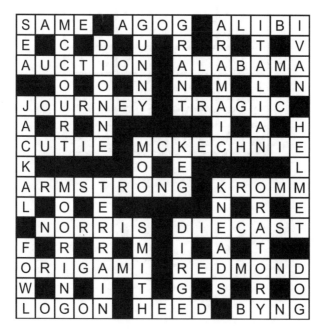

The 1970s – How well do you know them?

1. *He became the first player to record 1000 career assists.*
2. *Gil Perreault, who had just the set the record the year before*
3. *Dale McCourt*
4. *Buffalo Sabres and Vancouver Canucks*
5. *Eastern Division*
6. *The World Hockey Association*
7. *The 12-team league included the Alberta Oilers, Winnipeg Jets, Chicago Cougars, Houston Aeros, Los Angeles Sharks, Minnesota Fighting Saints, Cleveland Crusaders, New England Whalers, Quebec Nordiques, Ottawa Nationals, Philadelphia Blazers and the New York Raiders*
8. *The New York Islanders and the Atlanta Flames*
9. *31 goals — and he had 69 assists*
10. *The Montreal Canadiens*
11. *Eight years*
12. *Marcel Dionne*

Name That Red Wing

1. Nick Libett
2. Red Berenson
3. Mickey Redmond
4. Marcel Dionne
5. Gary Bergman
6. Jim Rutherford
7. Dennis Polonich
8. Dale McCourt
9. Vaclav Nedomansky
10. Reed Larson

Number 19

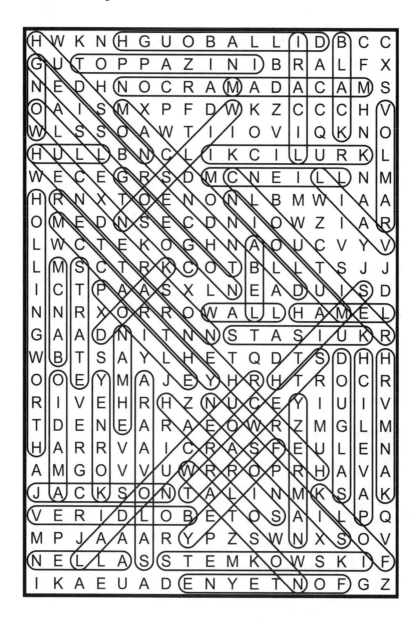

The 1980s

The 1980s – How well do you know them?

1. *Dale McCourt*
2. *John Ziegler, Jr. (1984), Keith Allen (1988) and Bud Poile (1989)*
3. *Brad Park*
4. *21*
5. *19 seasons/20 years*
6. *Winnipeg Jets*
7. *Joe Murphy*
8. *Jack Adams Award (1987,1988)*
9. *John A. Ziegler, Jr.*
10. *No*
11. *Bob Probert, 398 (1987-88)*

Yzerman Sudoku

Y	M	R	S	A	Z	N	E
E	N	Z	A	R	M	S	Y
Z	R	S	N	E	A	Y	M
A	Y	M	E	Z	S	R	N
M	A	N	Y	S	R	E	Z
R	S	E	Z	Y	N	M	A
N	E	A	R	M	Y	Z	S
S	Z	Y	M	N	E	A	R

Name That Red Wing

1. Mike Foligno
2. Willie Huber
3. Paul Woods
4. Danny Gare
5. John Ogrodnick
6. Greg Stefan
7. Gerard Gallant
8. Glen Hanlon
9. Shawn Burr
10. Steve Chiasson

Number 16

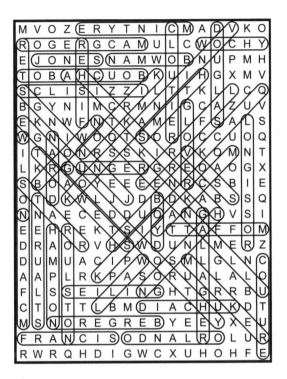

The 1990s

The 1990s – How well do you know them?

1. *Sergei Fedorov (1991), Nicklas Lidstrom (1992) and Vladimir Konstantinov (1992)*

2. *Paul Ysebaert (1991-92) and Vladimir Konstantinov (1995-96)*

3. *Team masseur Sergei Mnatsakanov (who was also seriously injured) and hockey player Viacheslav Fetisov (who recovered and was able to play again). If you knew the driver of the car was Richard Gnida, we're impressed.*

4. *The patch had the Red Wings logo with "Believe" written in both English and Russian below it. At the bottom were VK and SM to represent the two members of the Red Wing family who were injured between the seasons: Vladimir Konstantinov and Sergei Mnatsakanov.*

5. *The Left-Wing Lock System*

6. *He was traded to San Jose.*

7. *Steve Yzerman, who wasn't traded to San Jose the following season*

8. *Denis Potvin*

9. *Pittsburgh Penguins — February 8, 1997. The Red Wings won 6-5 in overtime.*

Stanley Cup Sudoku

T	Y	E	C	U	N	P	A	L	S
S	A	N	P	L	E	C	Y	T	U
L	N	P	S	C	Y	U	E	A	T
Y	U	T	A	E	L	N	S	C	P
E	P	A	L	T	U	S	N	Y	C
C	S	Y	U	N	A	T	P	E	L
P	L	C	N	Y	S	A	T	U	E
A	E	U	T	S	P	L	C	N	Y
U	T	S	Y	A	C	E	L	P	N
N	C	L	E	P	T	Y	U	S	A

Missing Wings

1. Steve Yzerman
2. Vladimir Konstantinov
3. Slava Kozlov
4. Sergei Fedorov
5. Mike Vernan
6. Chris Osgood
7. Darren McCarty
8. Igor Larionov
9. Larry Murphy
10. Brendan Shanahan
11. Nicklas Lidstrom

Missing Wings

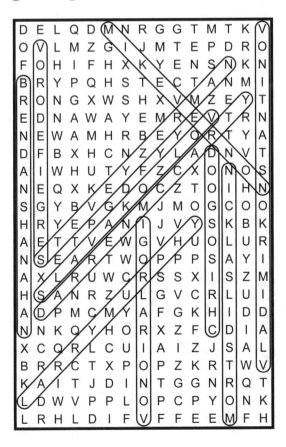

Trophy Winners in the 2000s

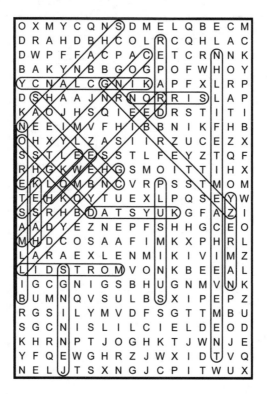

The 2000s

The 2000s – How well do you know them?

1. *Brendan Shanahan*

2. *Sergei Fedorov*

3. *The Winter Olympics took place in February in Salt Lake City, which is like an All-Star Game.*

4. *Vancouver Canucks, St. Louis Blues, Colorado Avalanche, Carolina Hurricanes*

5. *Dominik Hasek*

6. *Five— Nicklas Lidstorm, Mikael Samuelsson, Henrik Zetterberg, Nicklas Kronwall and Tomas Holmstrom.*

7. *Dominik Hasek*

8. *Mike Babcock*

9. *Scotty Bowman (2001), Marcel Dionne (2006), Reed Larson (2006), Red Berenson (2006), Steve Yzerman (2006), Ted Lindsay (2008), Jim Devellano (2009)*

10. *692*

"The Dominator" Sudoku

No Time Like the Present

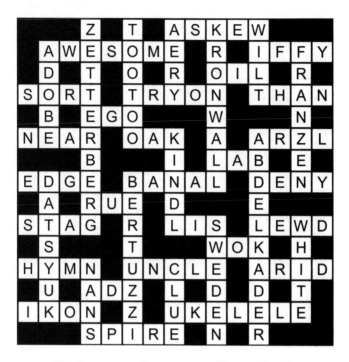

How well do you know Mike Ilitch?

1. *Cooley High School, Detroit, Michigan*
2. *U.S. Marine Corps*
3. *Second base*
4. *Little Caesars Pizza Treat in Garden City, Michigan*
5. *Seven – each own shares in the Red Wings and all have their names engraved on the Stanley Cup.*
6. *Fox Theatre – it is now the company headquarters.*

Red Wings' Stanley Cup Winning Years

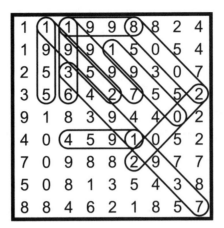

MY Team (Literally)

North American Red Wings

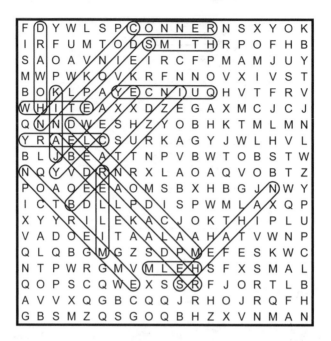

European Red Wings

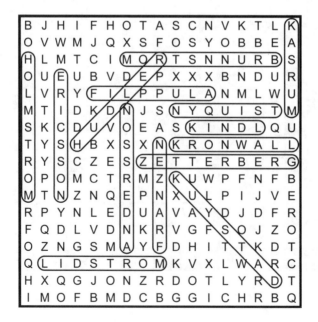

Hockey Films

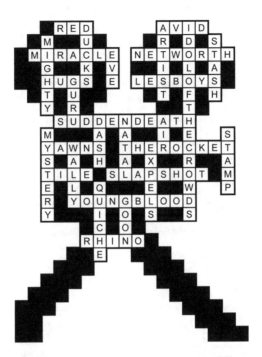

Coaches

Scotty Bowman Sudoku

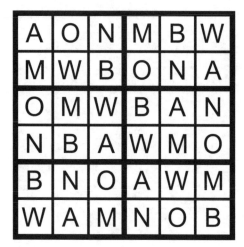

Bill Gadsby Sudoku

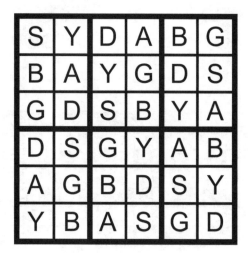

Find 'em All

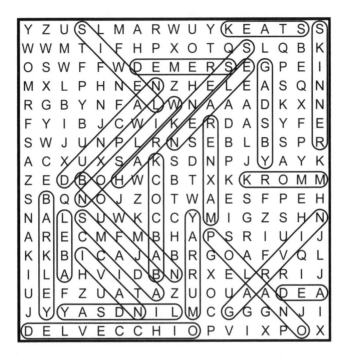

Also Known As

Todd Bertuzzi—Big Bert
Pavel Datsyuk—The Magic Man, Houdini
Alex Delvecchio—Fats
Marcel Dionne—Little Beaver
Dominik Hasek—Dominator
Gordie Howe—Mr. Hockey
Nicklas Lidstrom—Lids, The Perfect Human
Ted Lindsay—Terrible Ted
Henrik Zetterberg—Ice Berg, Zata
Steve Yzerman—Stevie Wonder, The Captain
Jack Stewart—Black Jack